STAR WARS® ADVENTURES

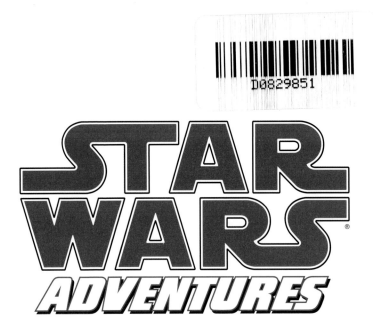

THE WILL OF DARTH VADER

Designer
Tony Ong

Assistant Editor
Freddye Lins

Editor
Randy Stradley

Publisher
Mike Richardson

special thanks to Jann Moorhead, David Anderman, Troy Alders, Leland Chee, Sue Rostoni, and
Carol Roeder at Lucas Licensing

STAR WARS ADVENTURES: THE WILL OF DARTH VADER

Published by
Dark Horse Books
A division of Dark Horse Comics, Inc.
10956 SE Main Street
Milwaukie, OR 97222

DarkHorse.com
StarWars.com

To find a comics shop in your area, call the Comic Shop Locator Service toll-free at 1-888-266-4226

Scholastic edition: July 2011
ISBN 978-1-59582-843-9

Printed at Solisco Printers, Ltd., Scott, QC, Canada

STAR WARS® ADVENTURES

THE WILL OF DARTH VADER

Script **Tom Taylor**

Pencils **Brian Koschak**

Inks **Dan Parsons**

Colors **Michael Wiggam**

Lettering **Michael Heisler**

Cover art **Sean McNally**

Dark Horse Books®

THIS STORY TAKES PLACE APPROXIMATELY THREE YEARS AFTER THE BATTLE OF YAVIN.

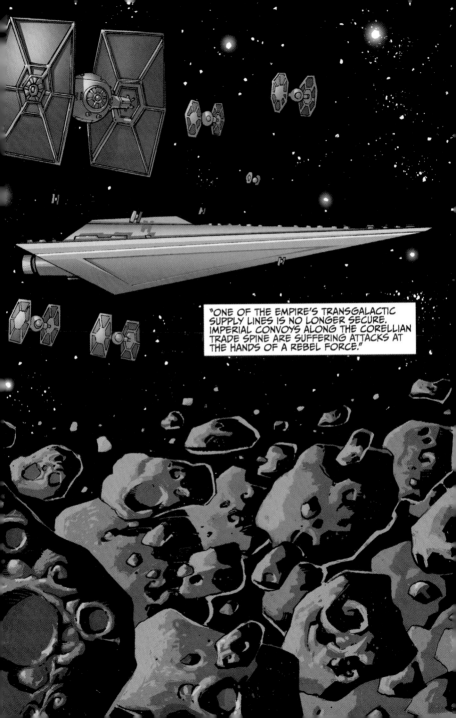

"ONE OF THE EMPIRE'S TRANSGALACTIC SUPPLY LINES IS NO LONGER SECURE. IMPERIAL CONVOYS ALONG THE CORELLIAN TRADE SPINE ARE SUFFERING ATTACKS AT THE HANDS OF A REBEL FORCE."

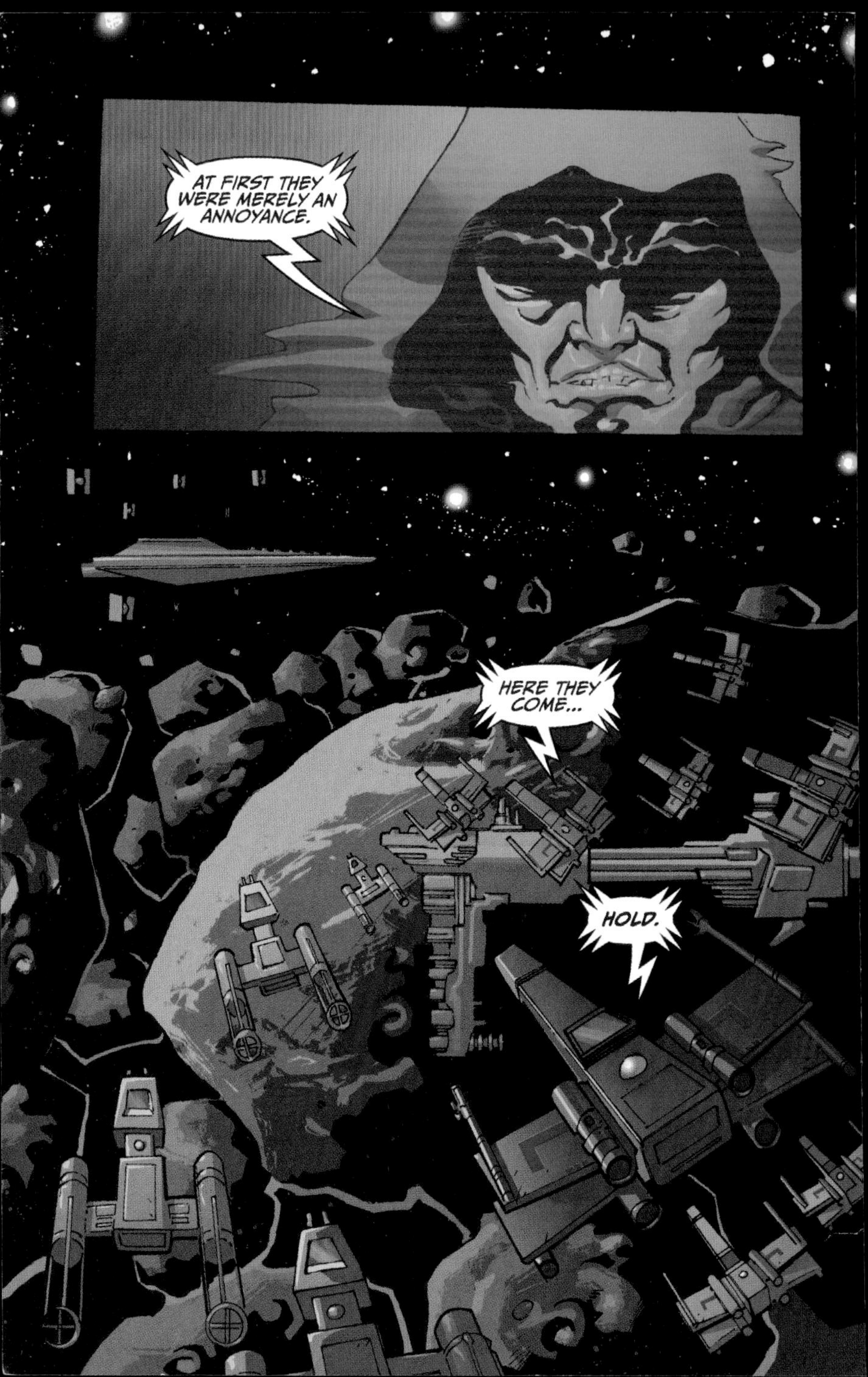
AT FIRST THEY WERE MERELY AN ANNOYANCE.
HERE THEY COME...
HOLD.

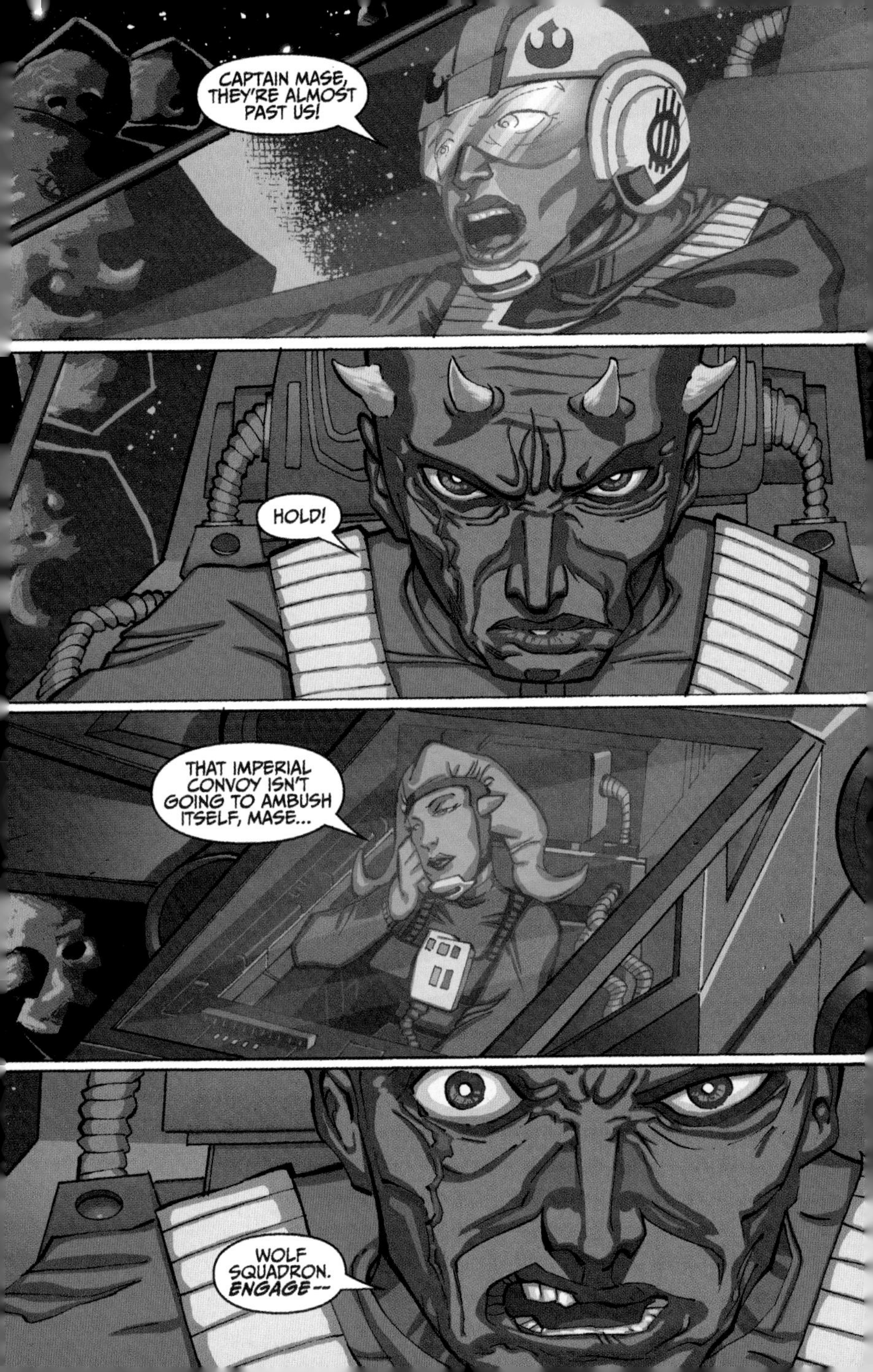

CAPTAIN MASE, THEY'RE ALMOST PAST US!
HOLD!
THAT IMPERIAL CONVOY ISN'T GOING TO AMBUSH ITSELF, MASE...
WOLF SQUADRON. *ENGAGE--*

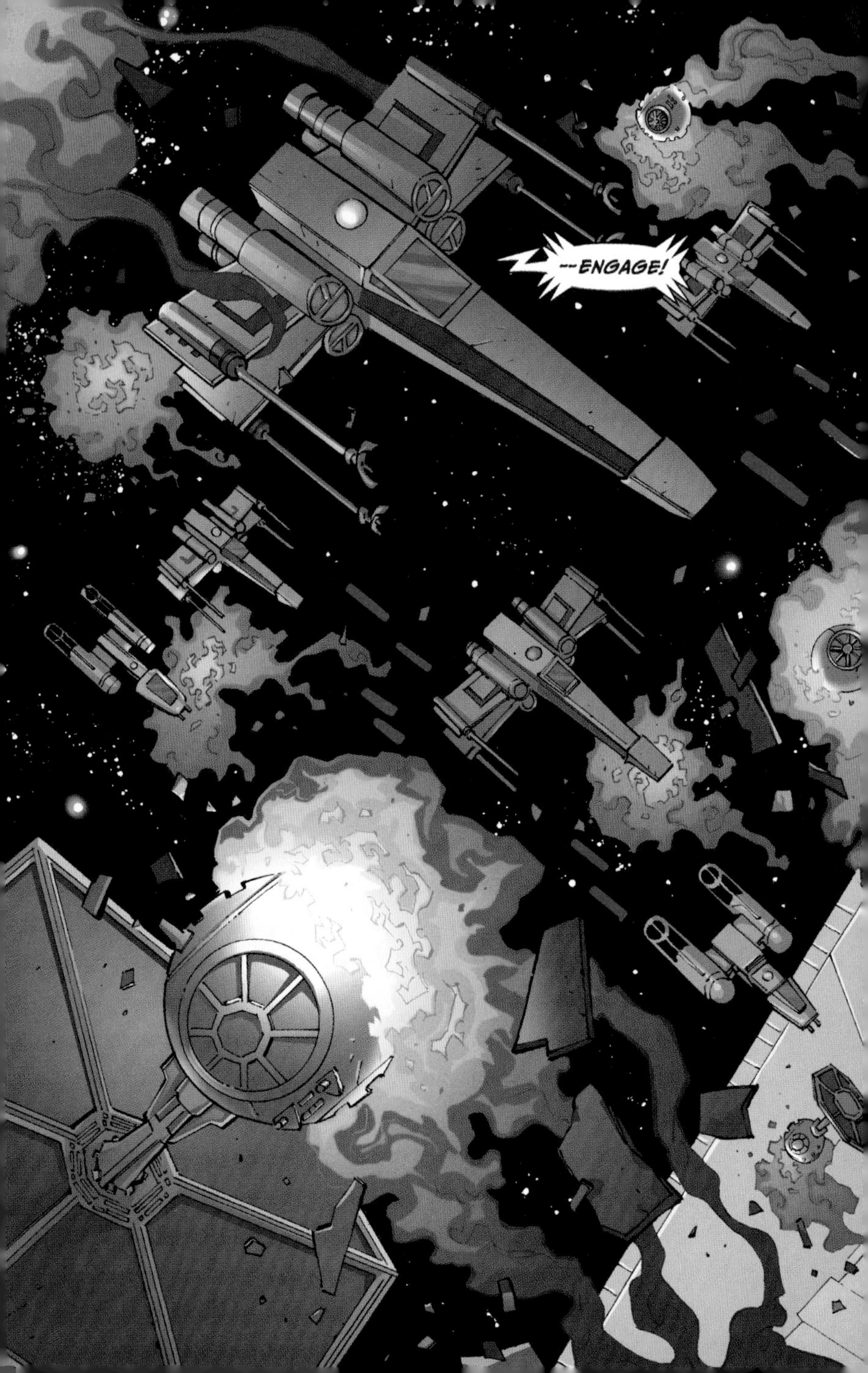
--ENGAGE!

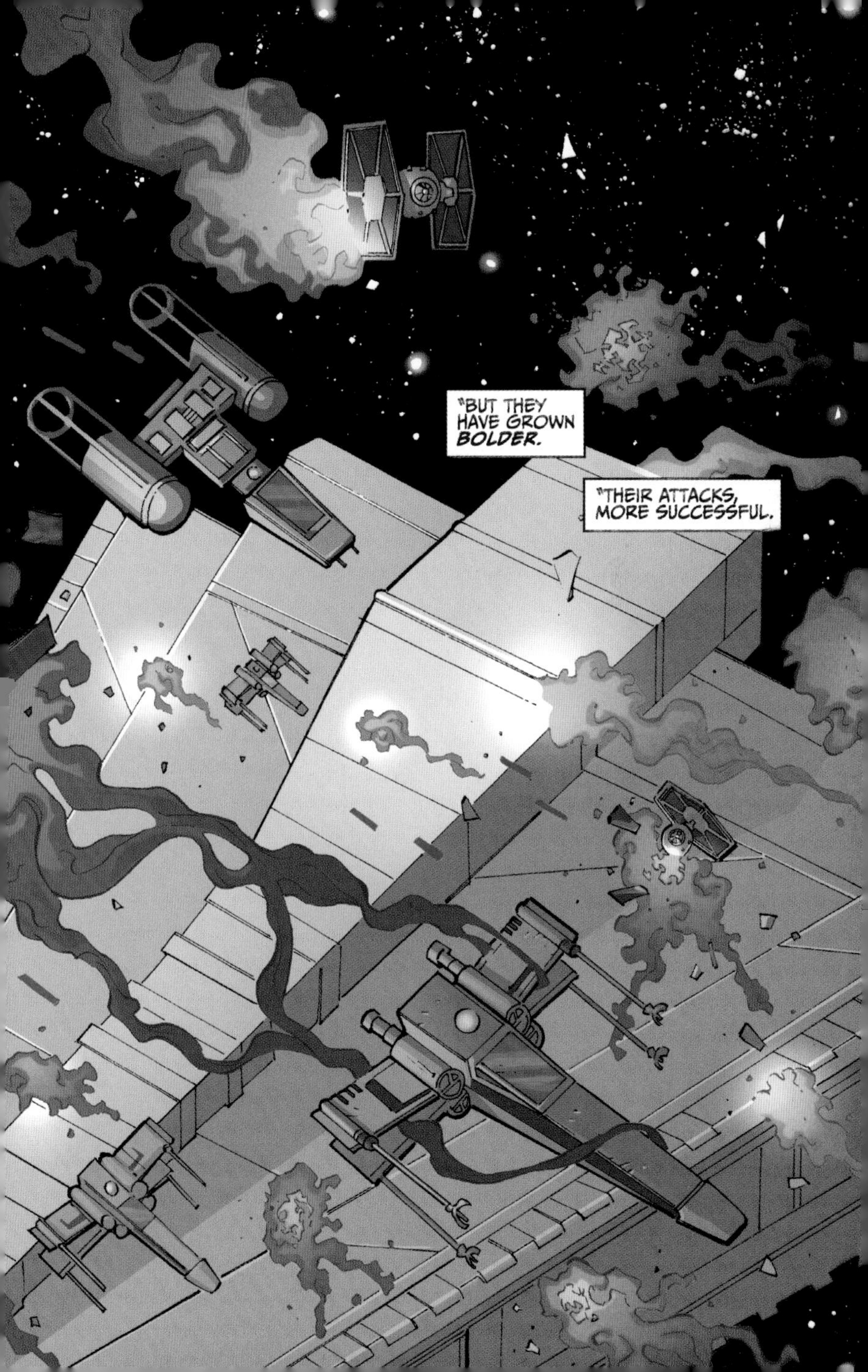
"BUT THEY HAVE GROWN BOLDER.
"THEIR ATTACKS, MORE SUCCESSFUL.

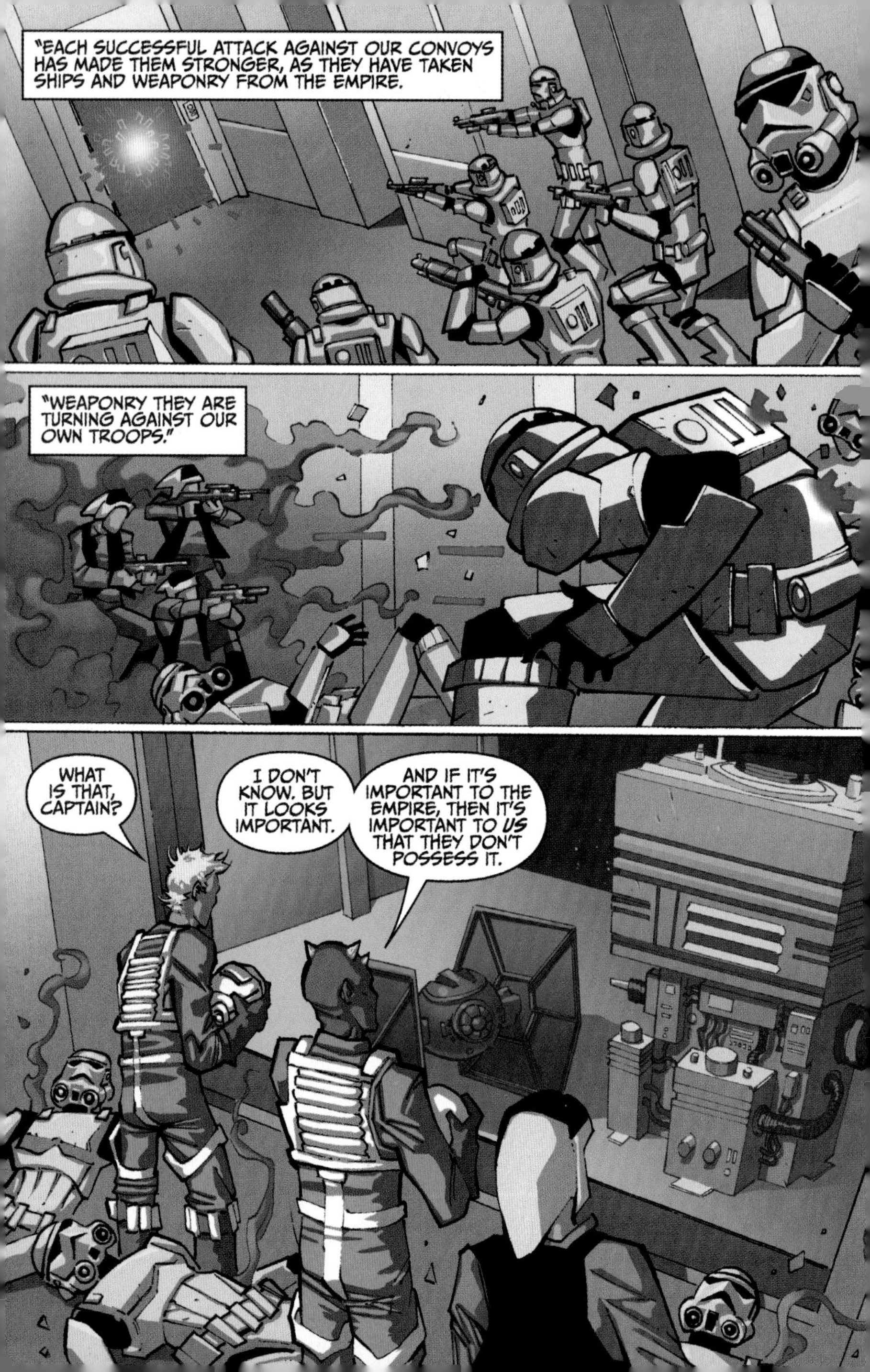
"EACH SUCCESSFUL ATTACK AGAINST OUR CONVOYS HAS MADE THEM STRONGER, AS THEY HAVE TAKEN SHIPS AND WEAPONRY FROM THE EMPIRE.
"WEAPONRY THEY ARE TURNING AGAINST OUR OWN TROOPS."
WHAT IS THAT, CAPTAIN?
I DON'T KNOW. BUT IT LOOKS IMPORTANT.
AND IF IT'S IMPORTANT TO THE EMPIRE, THEN IT'S IMPORTANT TO *US* THAT THEY DON'T *POSSESS* IT.

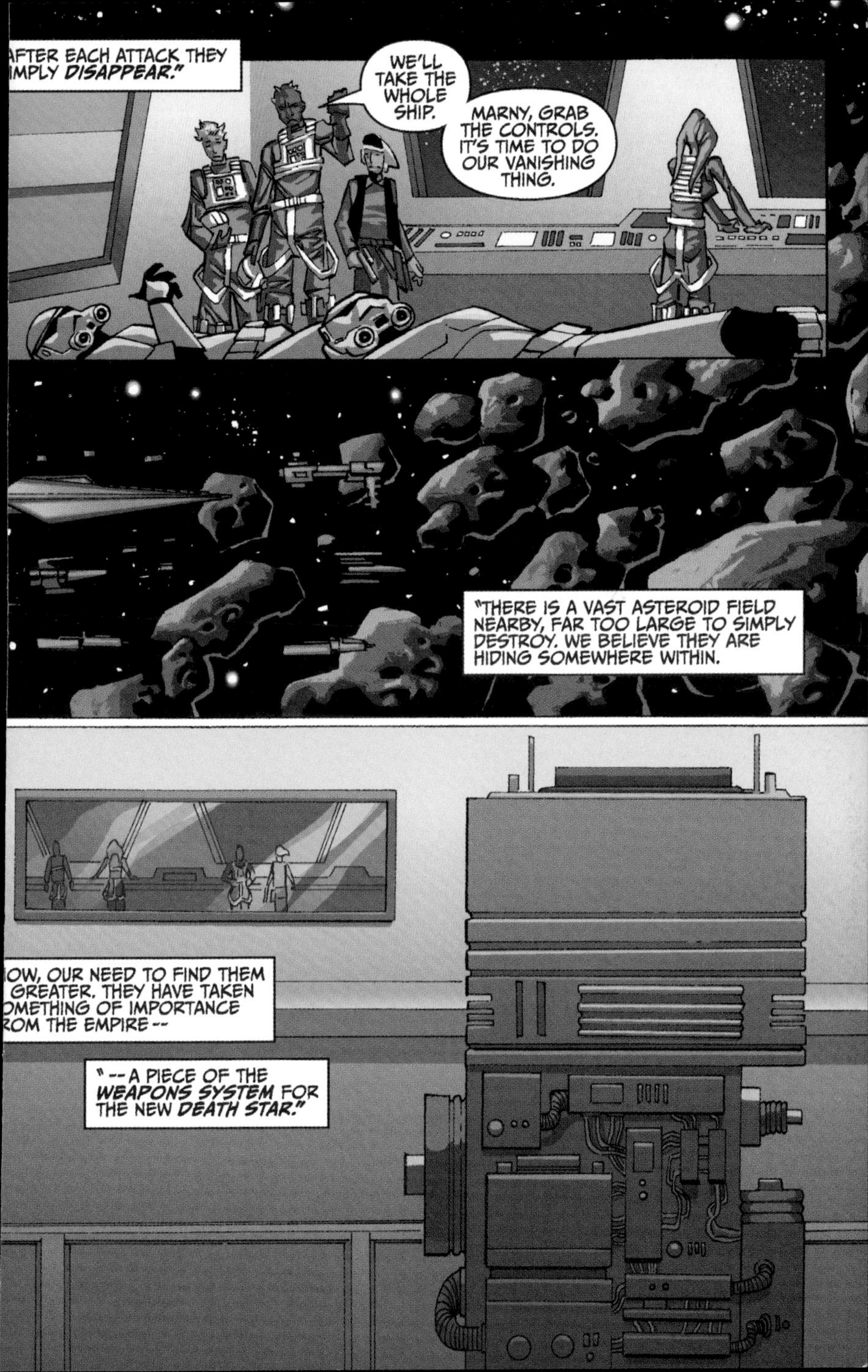
AFTER EACH ATTACK THEY SIMPLY *DISAPPEAR*."
WE'LL TAKE THE WHOLE SHIP.
MARNY, GRAB THE CONTROLS. IT'S TIME TO DO OUR VANISHING THING.
"THERE IS A VAST ASTEROID FIELD NEARBY, FAR TOO LARGE TO SIMPLY DESTROY. WE BELIEVE THEY ARE HIDING SOMEWHERE WITHIN.
NOW, OUR NEED TO FIND THEM GREATER. THEY HAVE TAKEN SOMETHING OF IMPORTANCE FROM THE EMPIRE --
" -- A PIECE OF THE *WEAPONS SYSTEM* FOR THE NEW *DEATH STAR*."

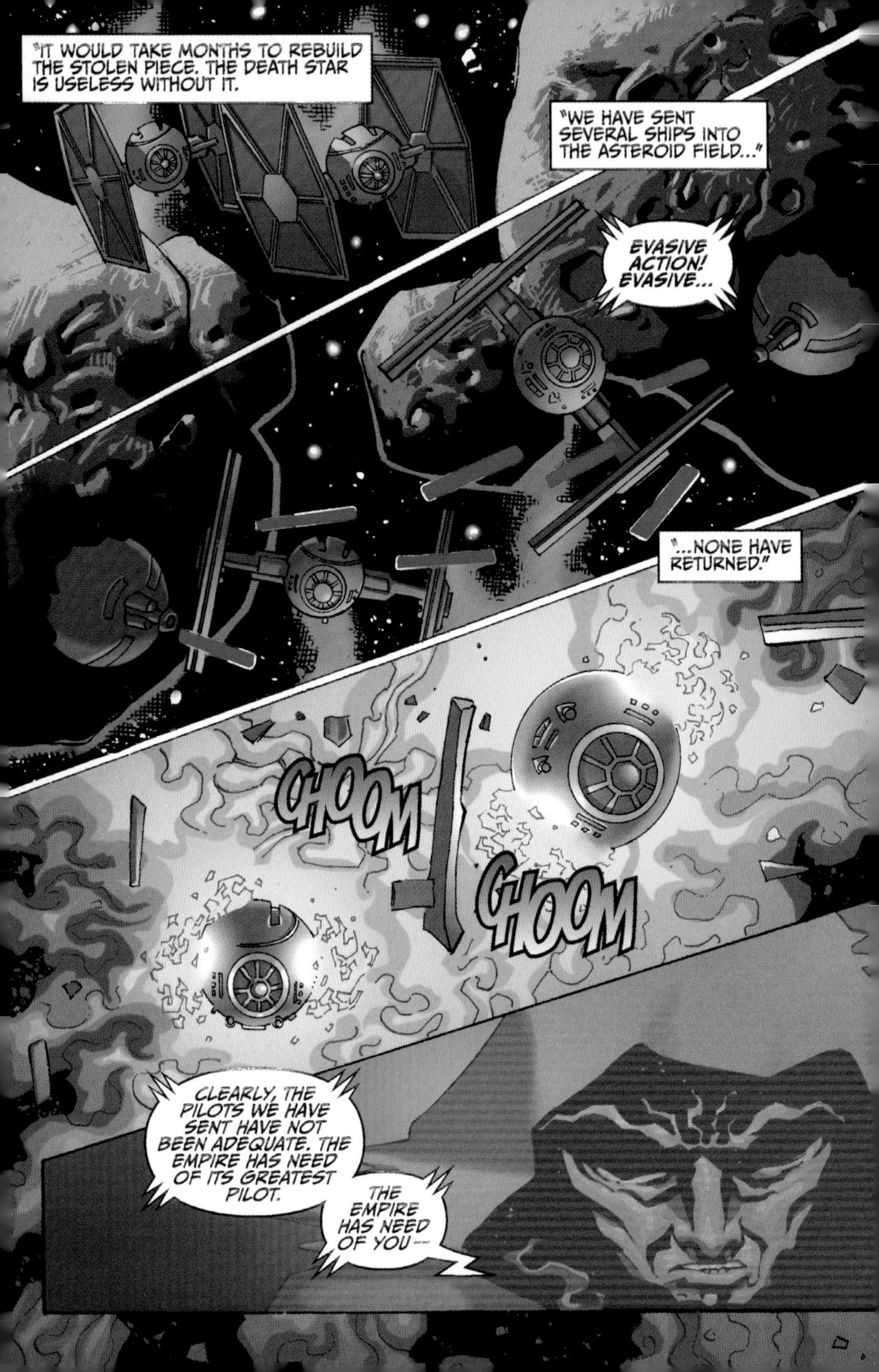
"IT WOULD TAKE MONTHS TO REBUILD THE STOLEN PIECE. THE DEATH STAR IS USELESS WITHOUT IT.
"WE HAVE SENT SEVERAL SHIPS INTO THE ASTEROID FIELD..."
EVASIVE ACTION! EVASIVE...
"...NONE HAVE RETURNED."
CHOOM
CHOOM
CLEARLY, THE PILOTS WE HAVE SENT HAVE NOT BEEN ADEQUATE. THE EMPIRE HAS NEED OF ITS GREATEST PILOT.
THE EMPIRE HAS NEED OF YOU

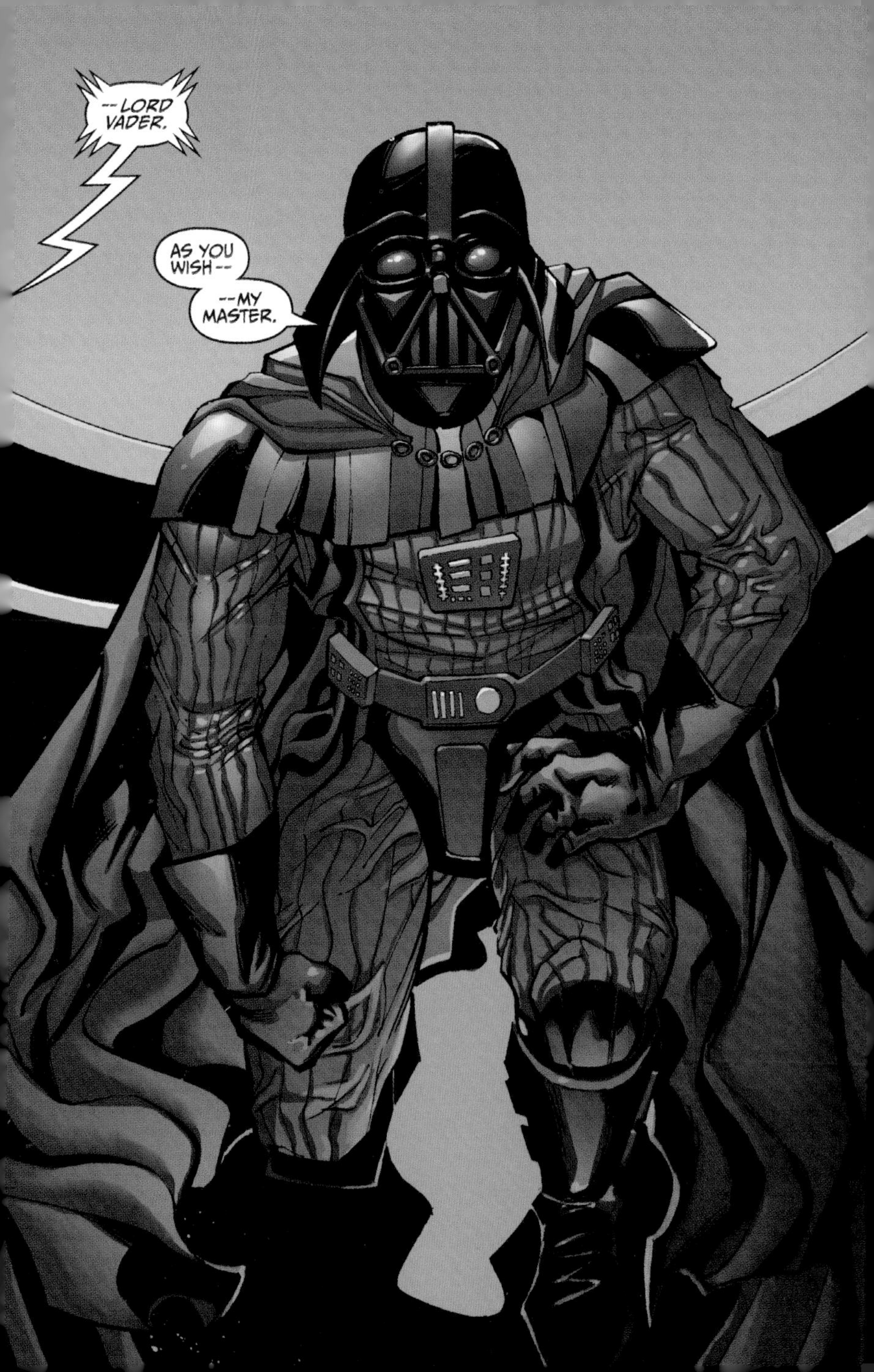
--LORD VADER.
AS YOU WISH--
--MY MASTER.

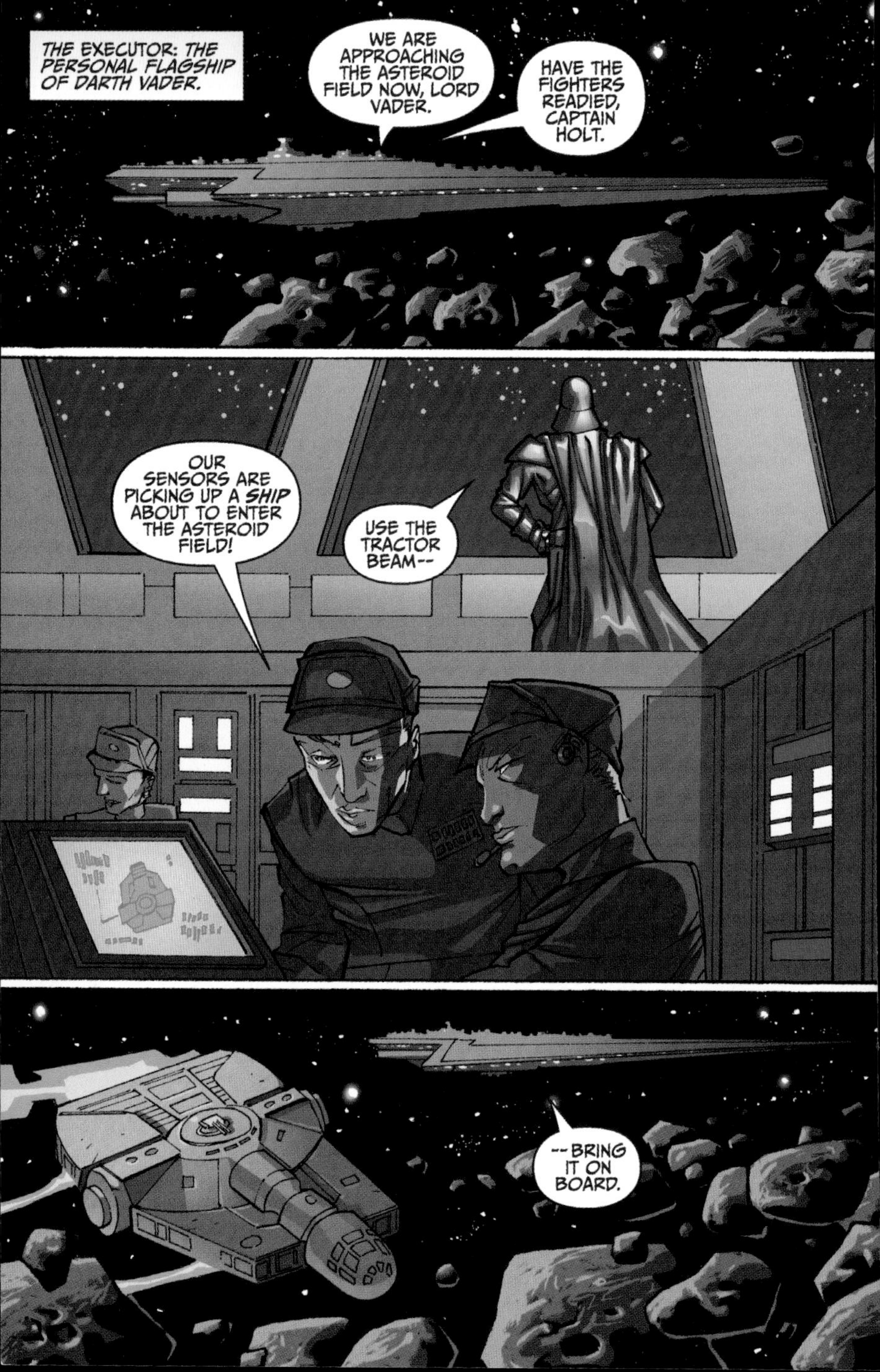
THE EXECUTOR: THE PERSONAL FLAGSHIP OF DARTH VADER.
WE ARE APPROACHING THE ASTEROID FIELD NOW, LORD VADER.
HAVE THE FIGHTERS READIED, CAPTAIN HOLT.
OUR SENSORS ARE PICKING UP A *SHIP* ABOUT TO ENTER THE ASTEROID FIELD!
USE THE TRACTOR BEAM--
--BRING IT ON BOARD.

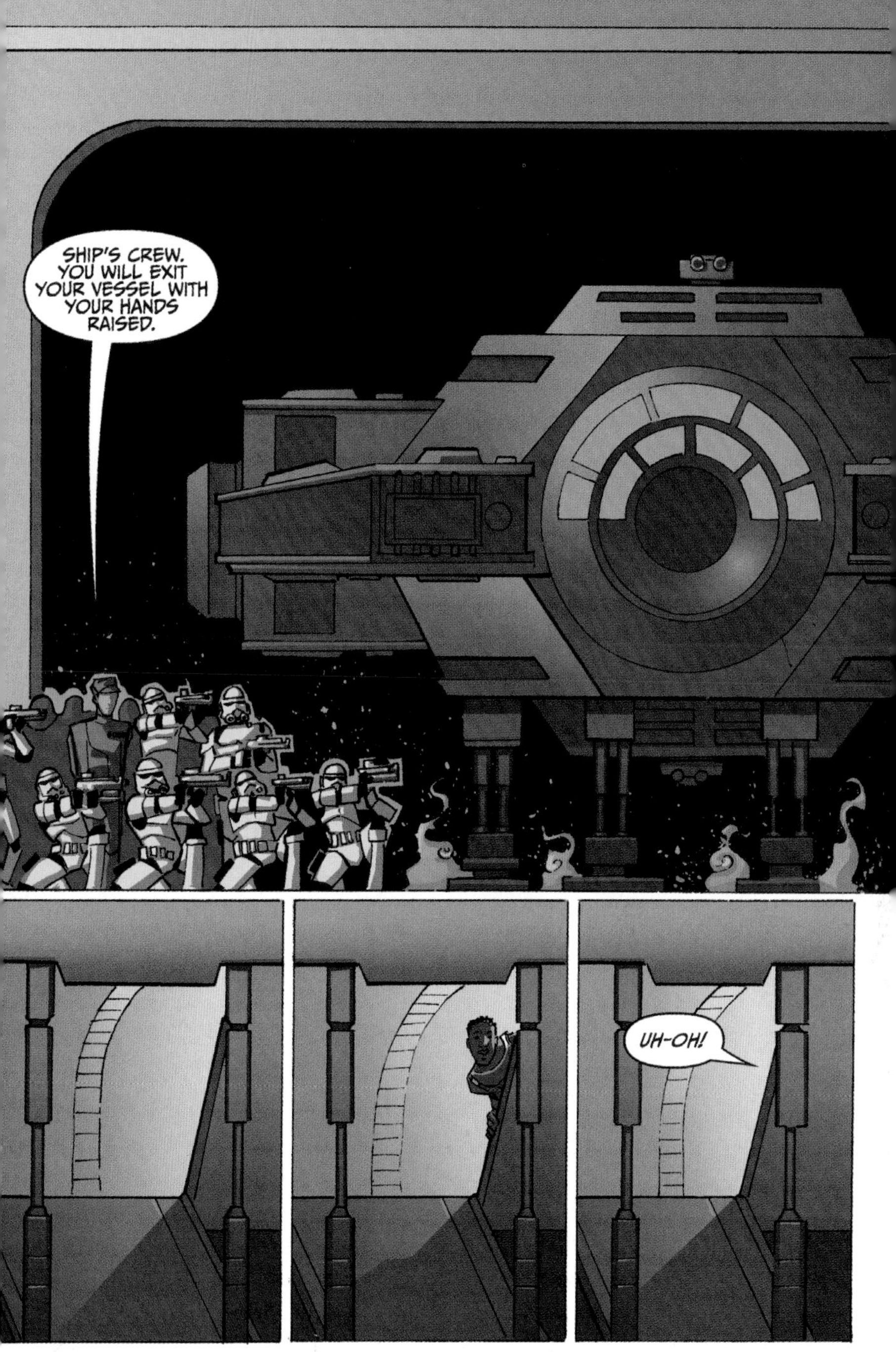
SHIP'S CREW. YOU WILL EXIT YOUR VESSEL WITH YOUR HANDS RAISED.
UH-OH!

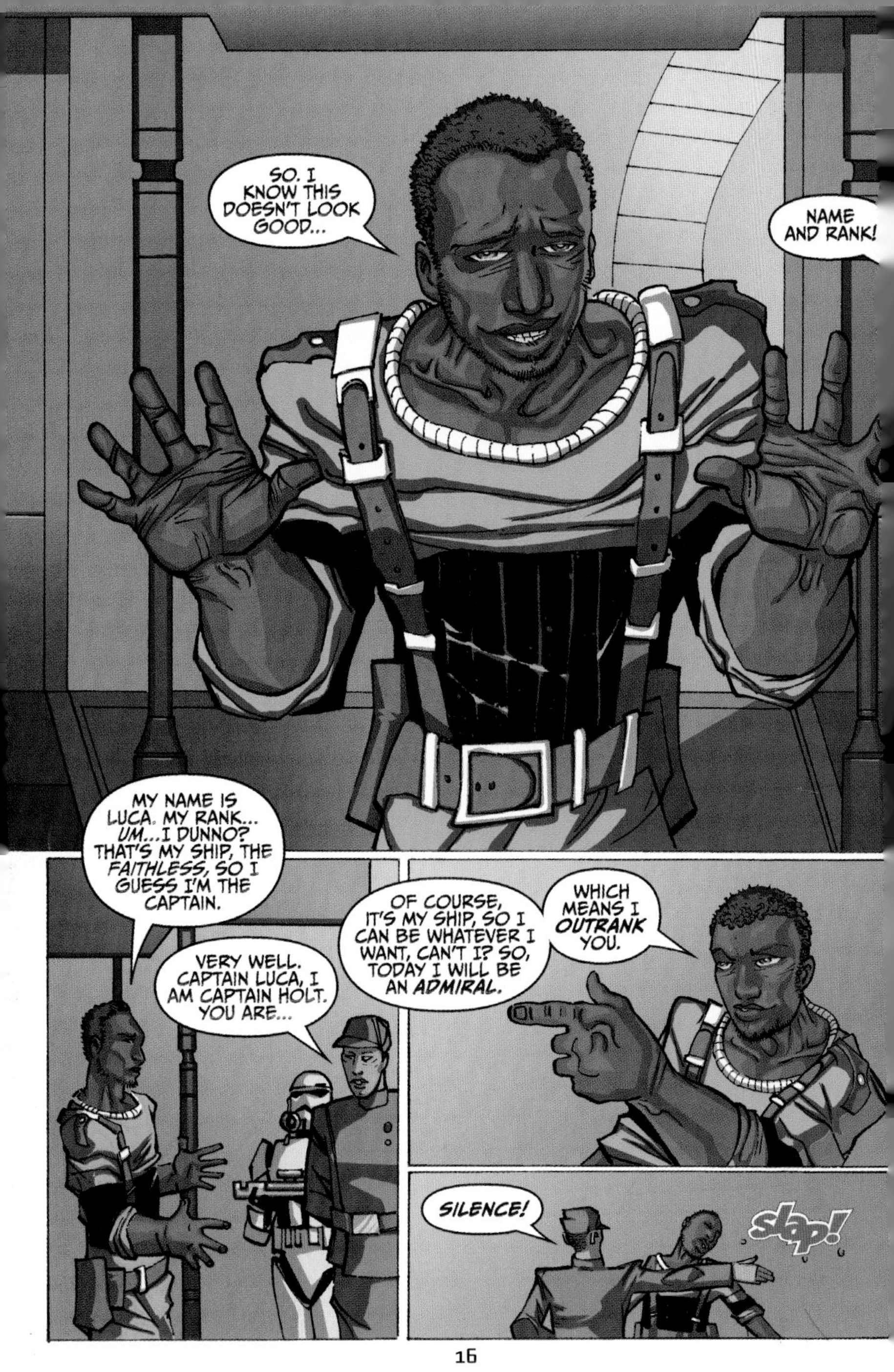
SO. I KNOW THIS DOESN'T LOOK GOOD...
NAME AND RANK!
MY NAME IS LUCA. MY RANK... *UM*...I DUNNO? THAT'S MY SHIP, THE *FAITHLESS*, SO I GUESS I'M THE CAPTAIN.
VERY WELL. CAPTAIN LUCA, I AM CAPTAIN HOLT. YOU ARE...
OF COURSE, IT'S MY SHIP, SO I CAN BE WHATEVER I WANT, CAN'T I? SO, TODAY I WILL BE AN *ADMIRAL*.
WHICH MEANS I *OUTRANK* YOU.
SILENCE!
SLAP!

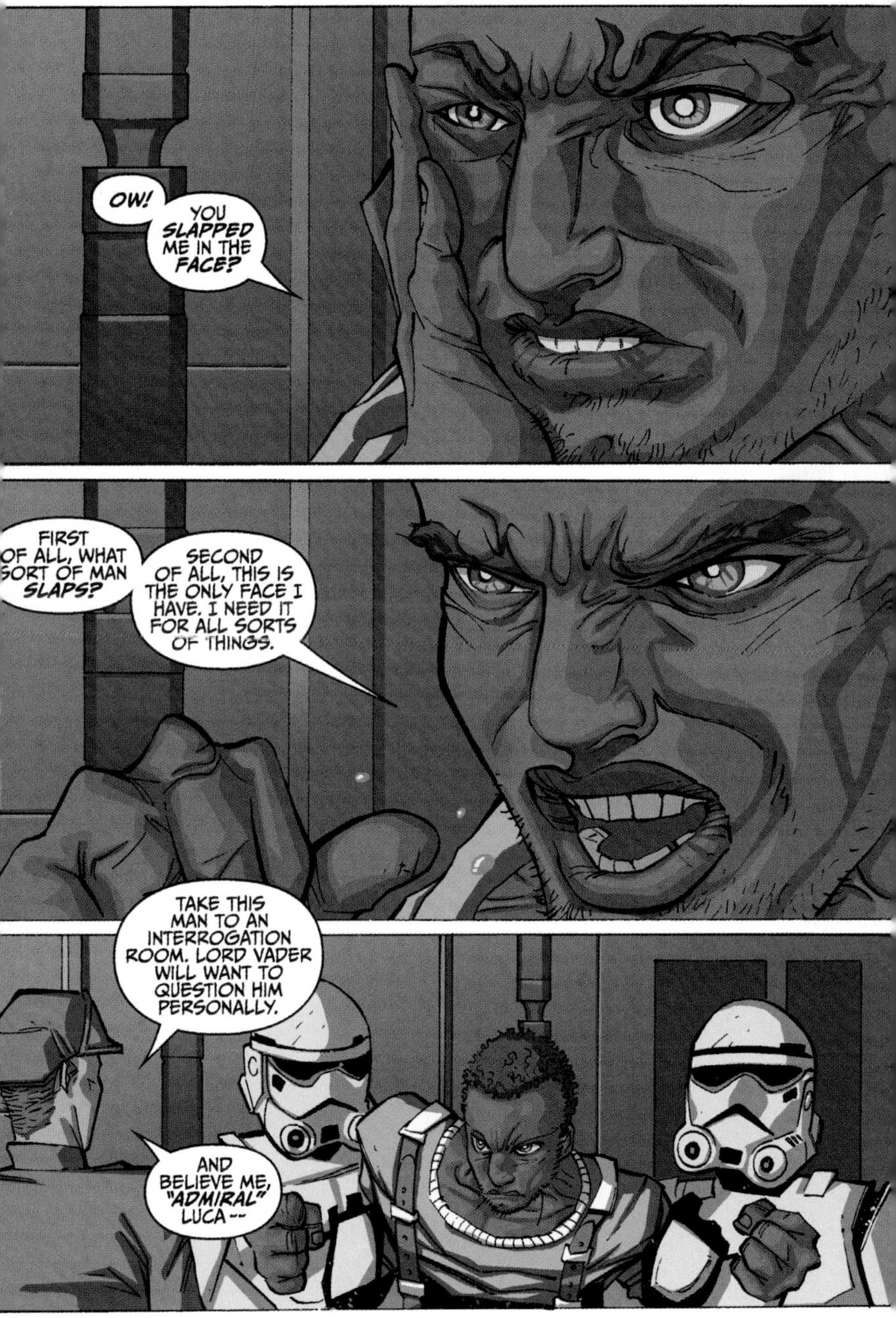
OW!
YOU SLAPPED ME IN THE FACE?
FIRST OF ALL, WHAT SORT OF MAN SLAPS?
SECOND OF ALL, THIS IS THE ONLY FACE I HAVE. I NEED IT FOR ALL SORTS OF THINGS.
TAKE THIS MAN TO AN INTERROGATION ROOM. LORD VADER WILL WANT TO QUESTION HIM PERSONALLY.
AND BELIEVE ME, "ADMIRAL" LUCA--

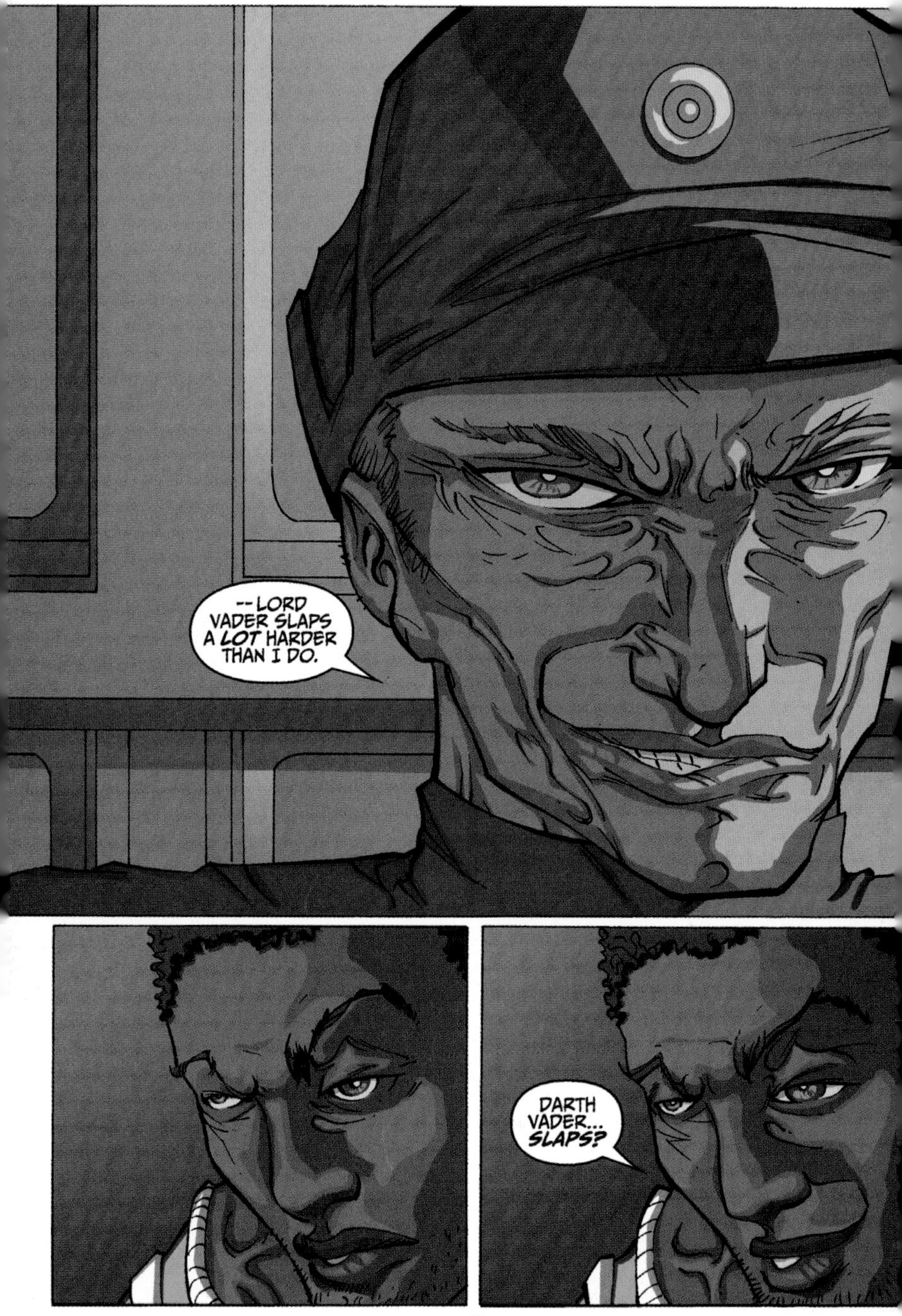
--LORD VADER SLAPS A *LOT* HARDER THAN I DO.
DARTH VADER... *SLAPS?*

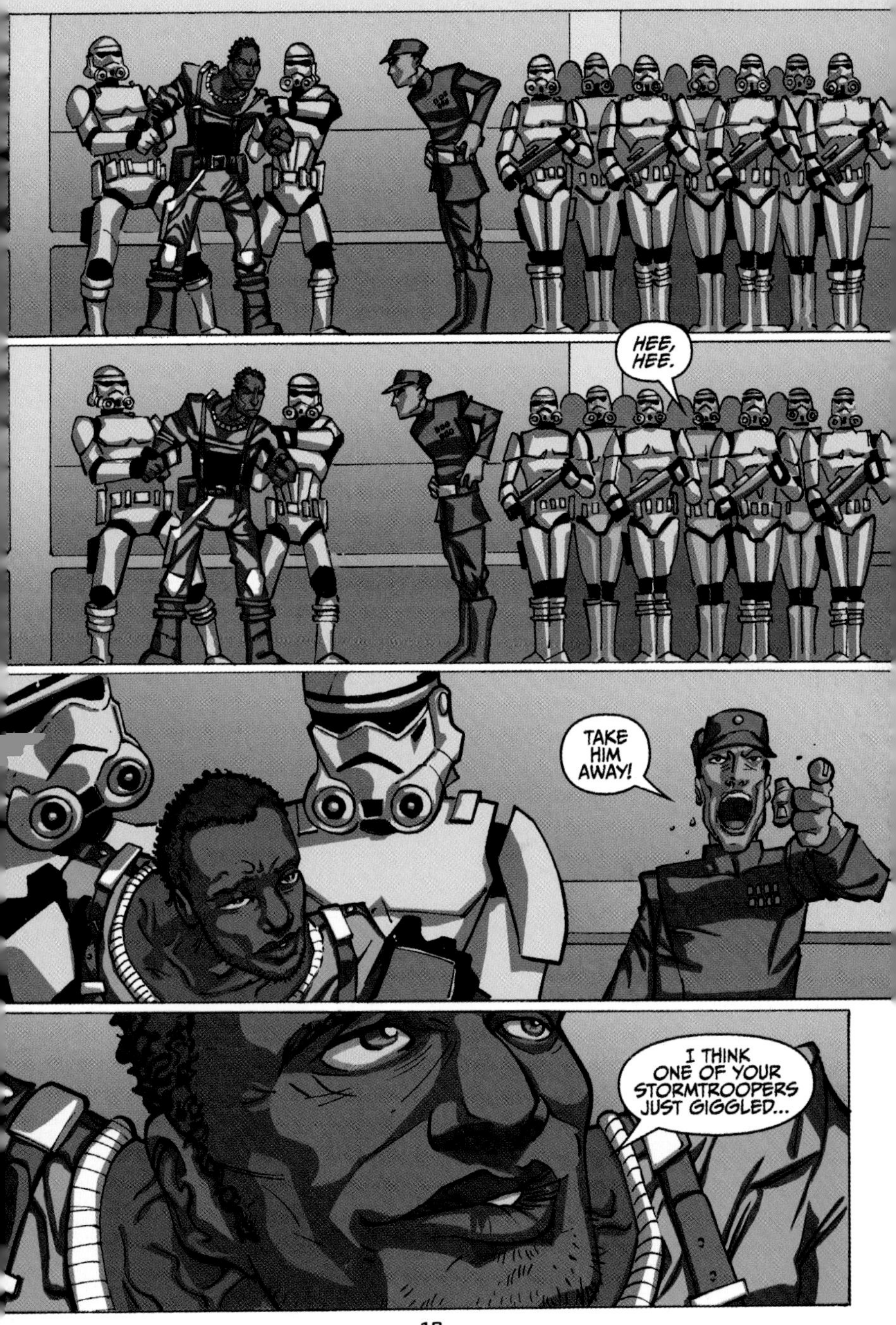
HEE, HEE.
TAKE HIM AWAY!
I THINK ONE OF YOUR STORMTROOPERS JUST GIGGLED...

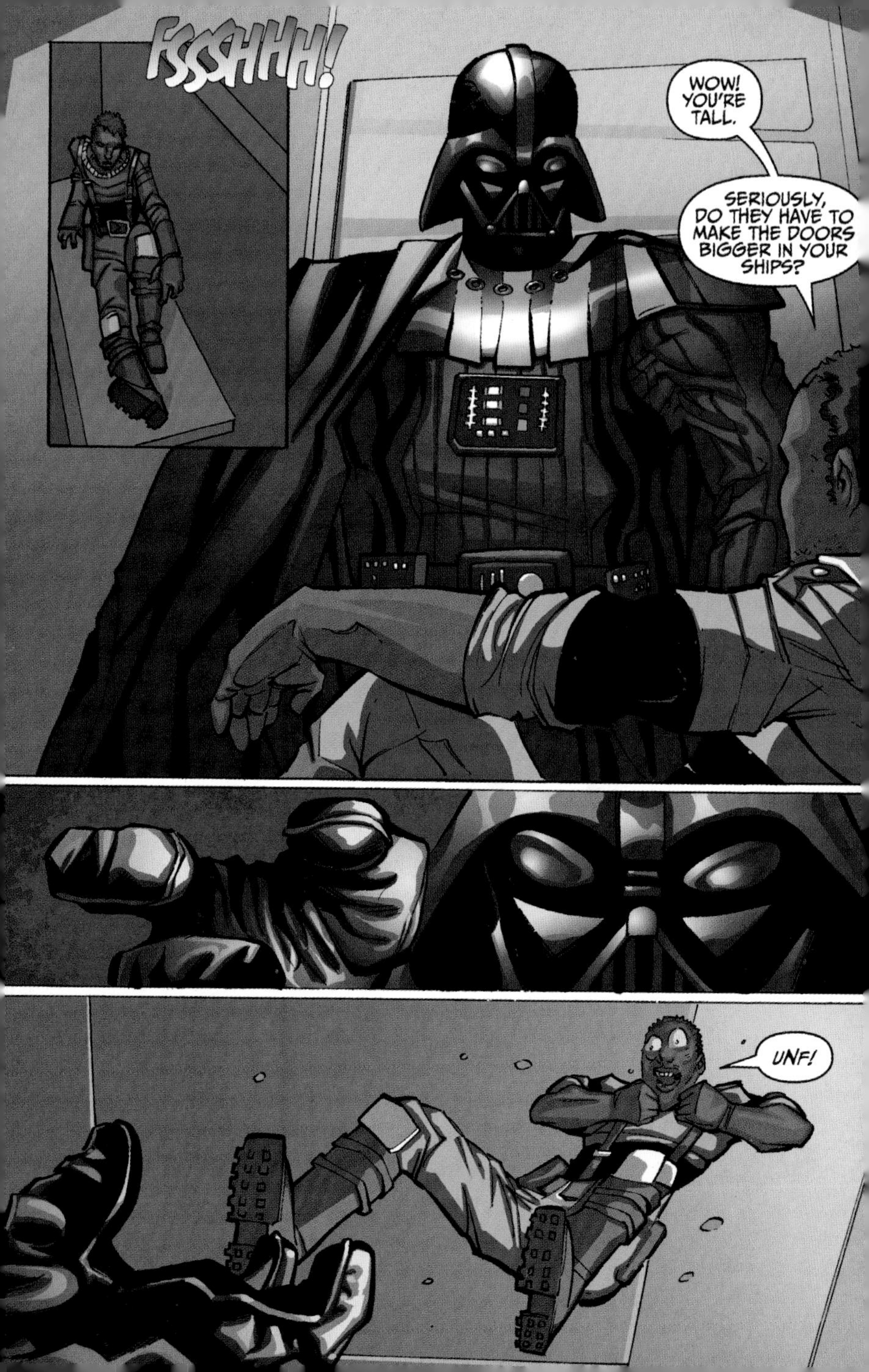
FSSSHHH!
WOW! YOU'RE TALL.
SERIOUSLY, DO THEY HAVE TO MAKE THE DOORS BIGGER IN YOUR SHIPS?
UNF!

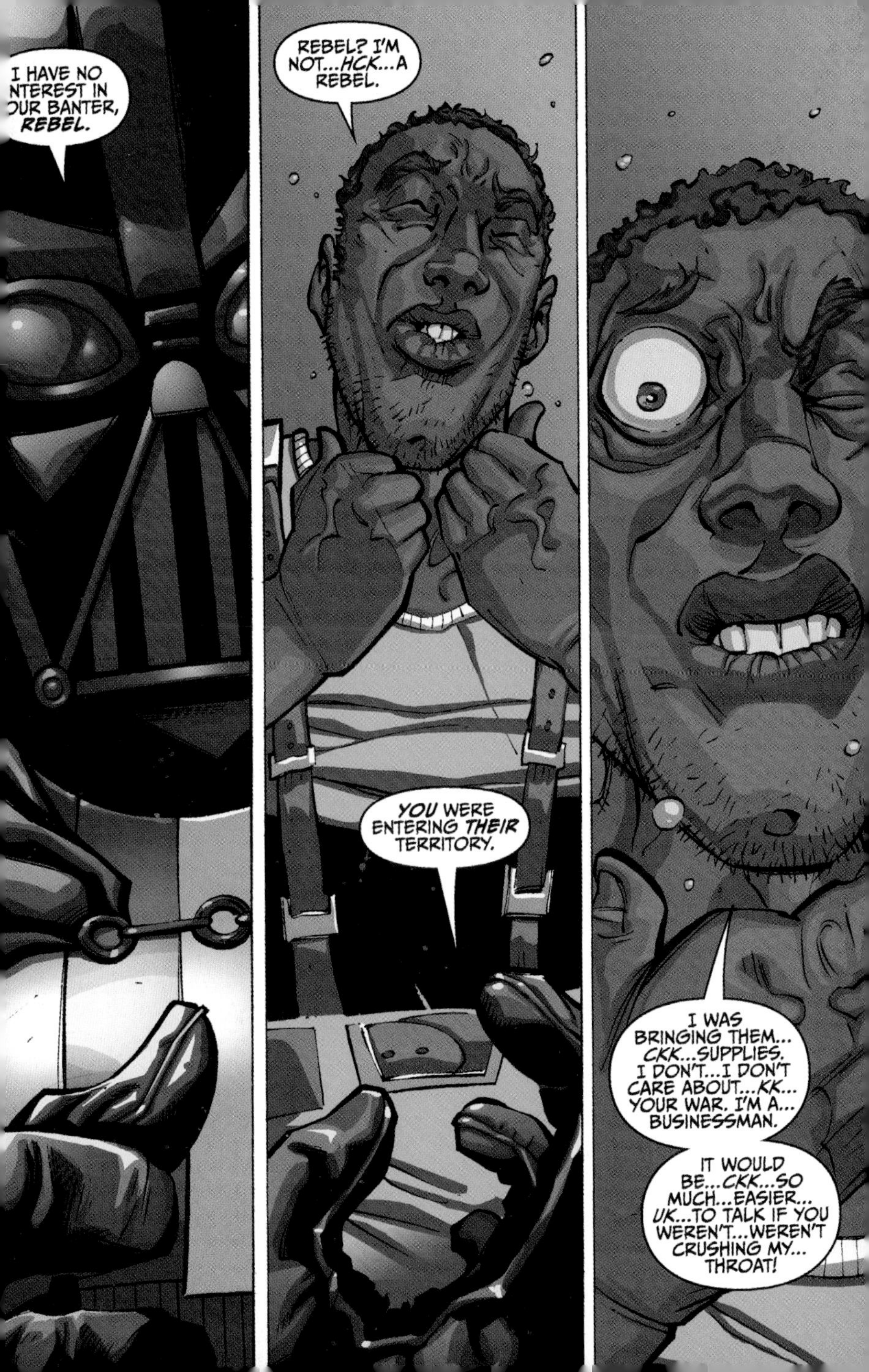
I HAVE NO
NTEREST IN
OUR BANTER,
REBEL.
REBEL? I'M
NOT...*HCK*...A
REBEL.
YOU WERE
ENTERING *THEIR*
TERRITORY.
I WAS
BRINGING THEM...
CKK...SUPPLIES.
I DON'T...I DON'T
CARE ABOUT...*KK*...
YOUR WAR. I'M A...
BUSINESSMAN.
IT WOULD
BE...*CKK*...SO
MUCH...EASIER...
UK...TO TALK IF YOU
WEREN'T...WEREN'T
CRUSHING MY...
THROAT!

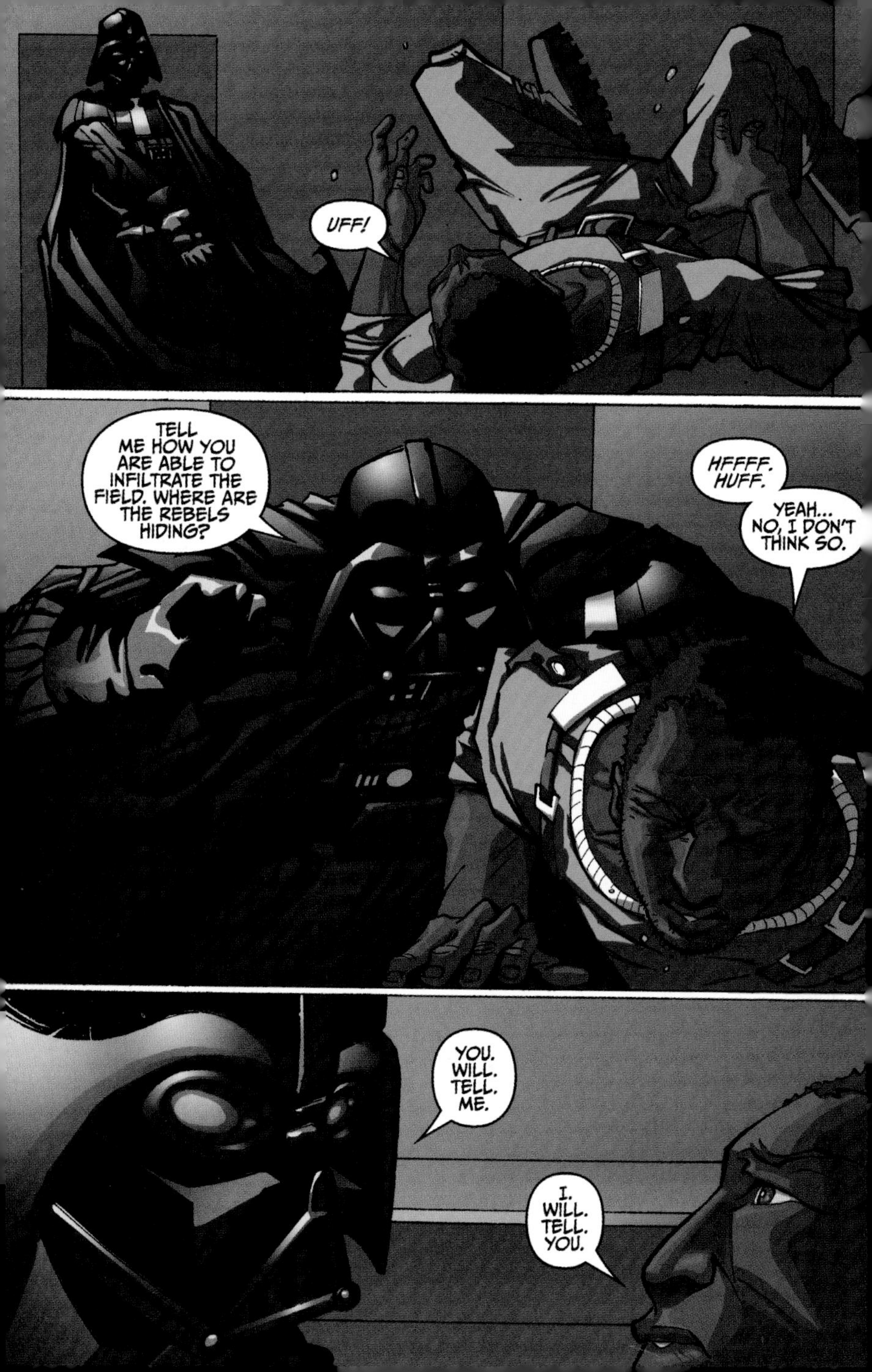
UFF!
TELL ME HOW YOU ARE ABLE TO INFILTRATE THE FIELD. WHERE ARE THE REBELS HIDING?
HFFFF. HUFF.
YEAH... NO, I DON'T THINK SO.
YOU. WILL. TELL. ME.
I. WILL. TELL. YOU.

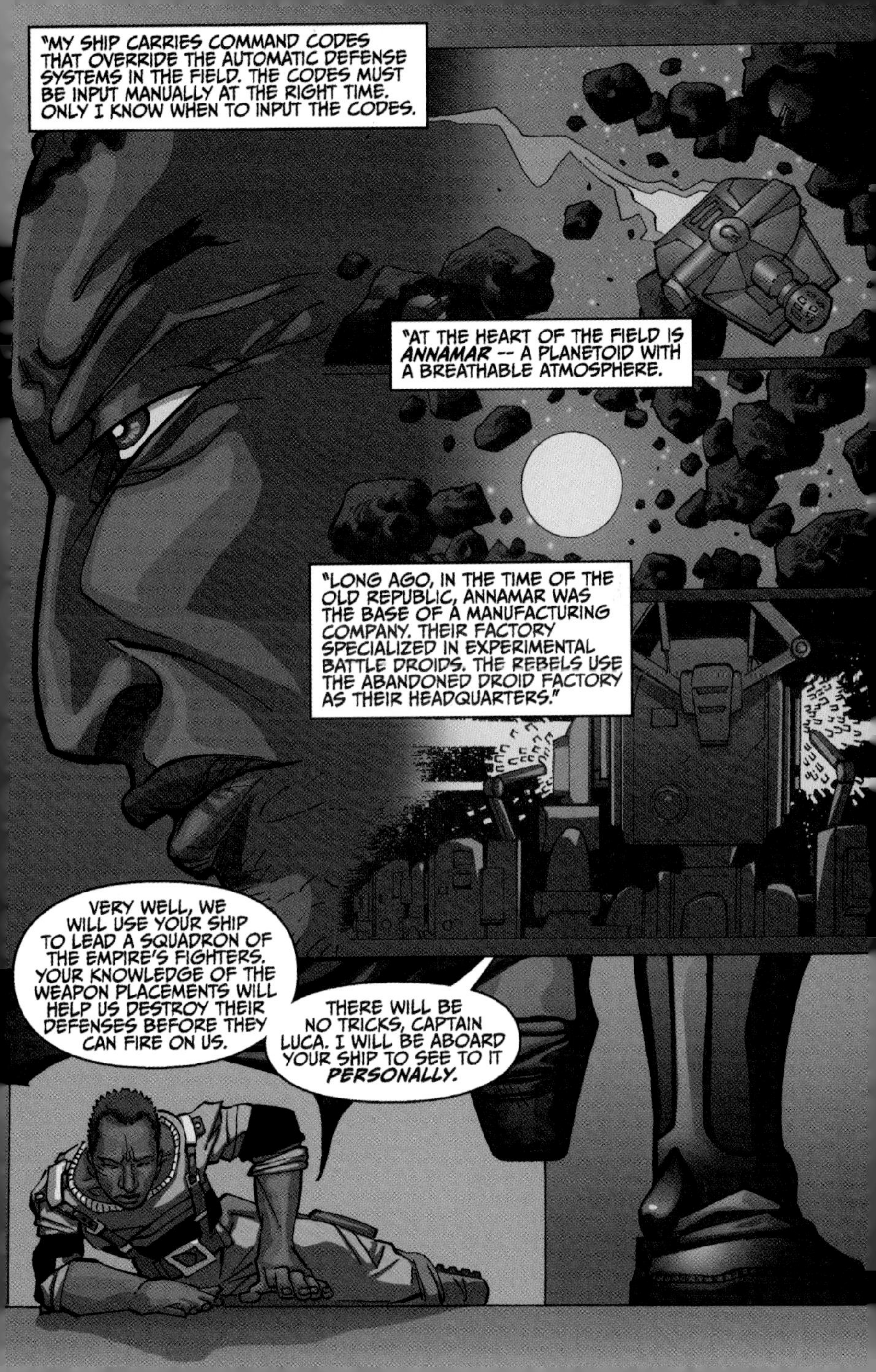
"MY SHIP CARRIES COMMAND CODES THAT OVERRIDE THE AUTOMATIC DEFENSE SYSTEMS IN THE FIELD. THE CODES MUST BE INPUT MANUALLY AT THE RIGHT TIME. ONLY I KNOW WHEN TO INPUT THE CODES.
"AT THE HEART OF THE FIELD IS ANNAMAR -- A PLANETOID WITH A BREATHABLE ATMOSPHERE.
"LONG AGO, IN THE TIME OF THE OLD REPUBLIC, ANNAMAR WAS THE BASE OF A MANUFACTURING COMPANY. THEIR FACTORY SPECIALIZED IN EXPERIMENTAL BATTLE DROIDS. THE REBELS USE THE ABANDONED DROID FACTORY AS THEIR HEADQUARTERS."
VERY WELL, WE WILL USE YOUR SHIP TO LEAD A SQUADRON OF THE EMPIRE'S FIGHTERS. YOUR KNOWLEDGE OF THE WEAPON PLACEMENTS WILL HELP US DESTROY THEIR DEFENSES BEFORE THEY CAN FIRE ON US.
THERE WILL BE NO TRICKS, CAPTAIN LUCA. I WILL BE ABOARD YOUR SHIP TO SEE TO IT PERSONALLY.

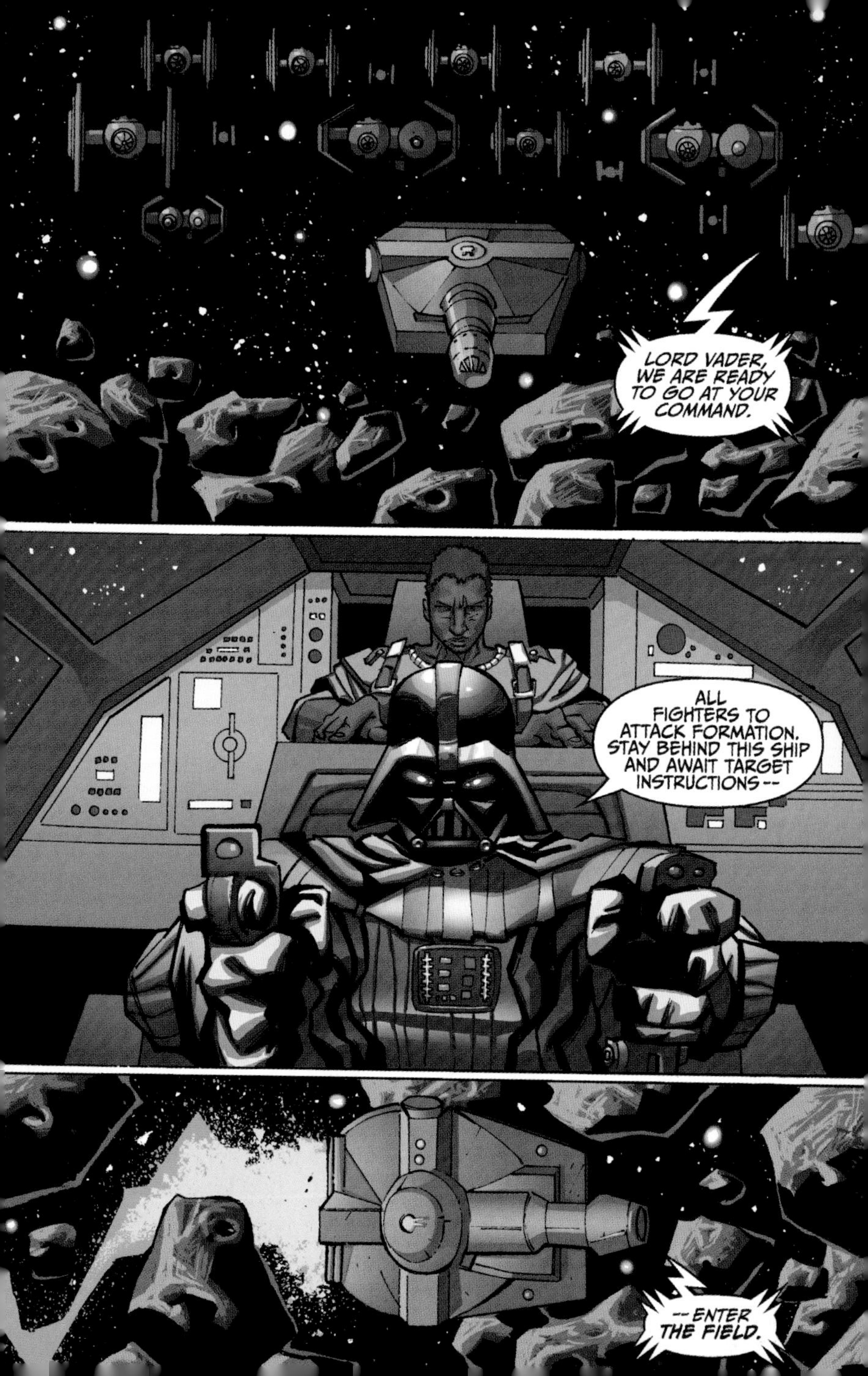
LORD VADER, WE ARE READY TO GO AT YOUR COMMAND.
ALL FIGHTERS TO ATTACK FORMATION. STAY BEHIND THIS SHIP AND AWAIT TARGET INSTRUCTIONS--
--ENTER THE FIELD.

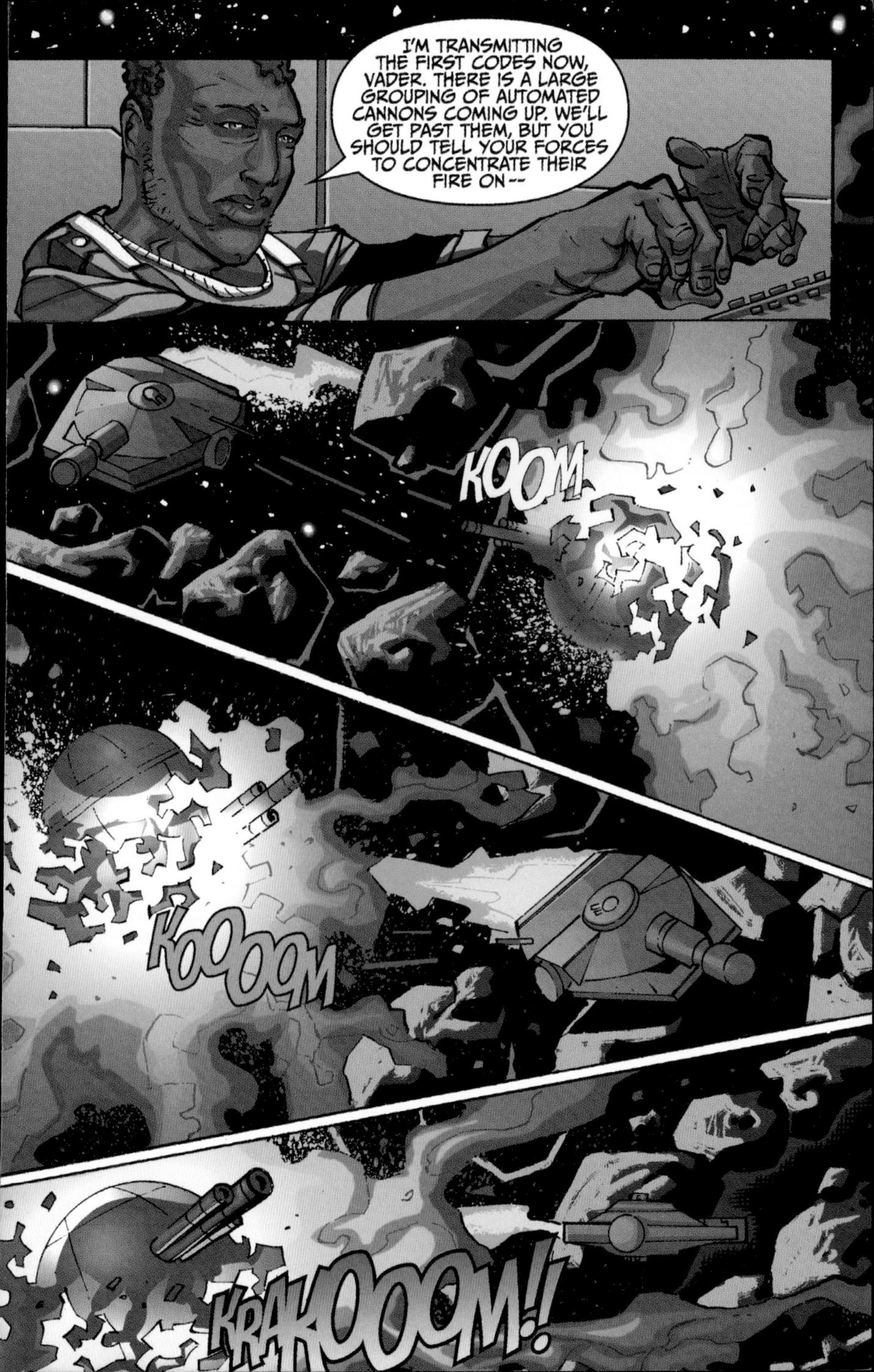
I'M TRANSMITTING THE FIRST CODES NOW, VADER. THERE IS A LARGE GROUPING OF AUTOMATED CANNONS COMING UP. WE'LL GET PAST THEM, BUT YOU SHOULD TELL YOUR FORCES TO CONCENTRATE THEIR FIRE ON--
KOOM
KOOOOM
KRAKOOOM!!

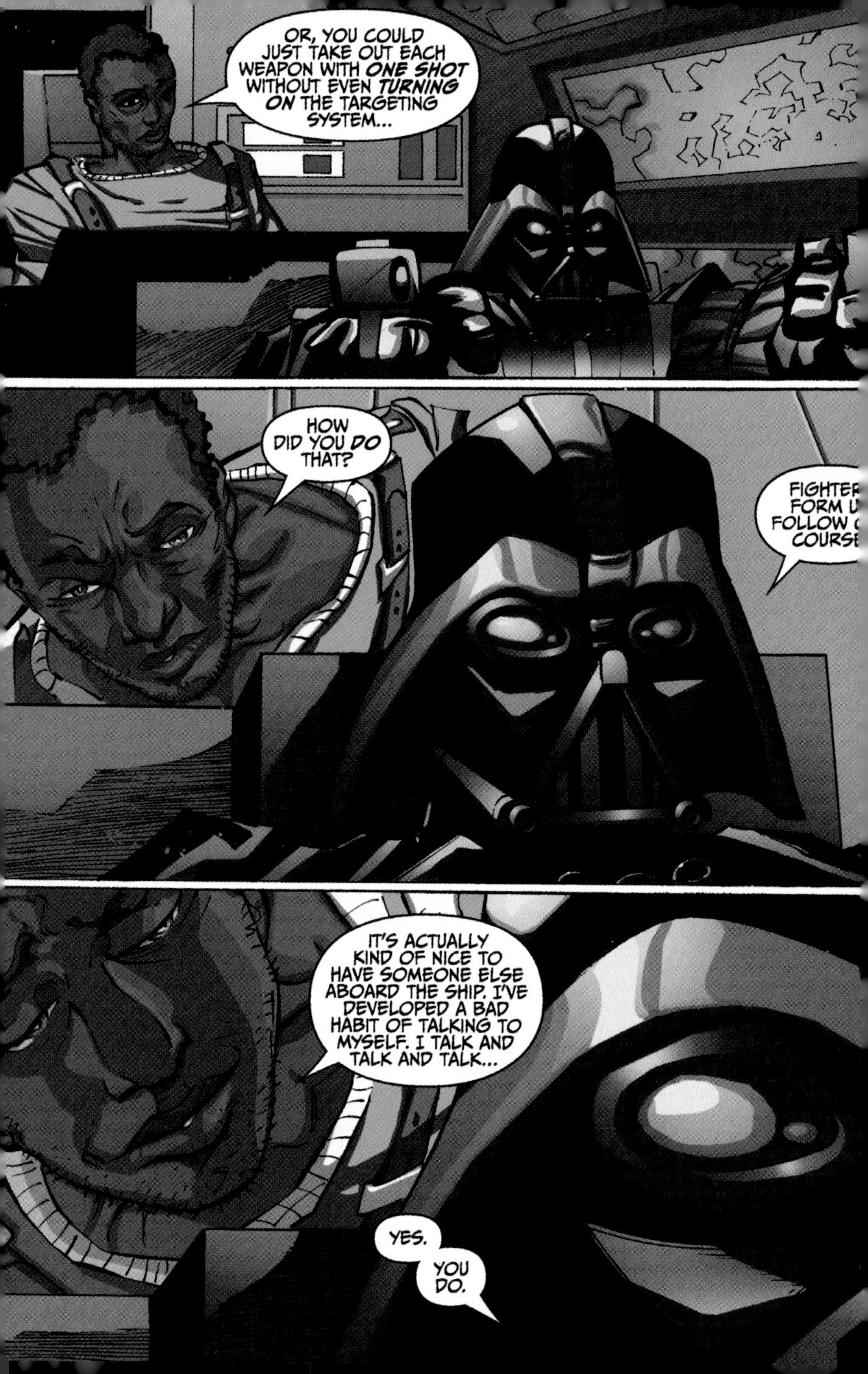
OR, YOU COULD JUST TAKE OUT EACH WEAPON WITH *ONE SHOT* WITHOUT EVEN *TURNING ON* THE TARGETING SYSTEM...
HOW DID YOU *DO* THAT?
FIGHTER FORM FOLLOW COURSE
IT'S ACTUALLY KIND OF NICE TO HAVE SOMEONE ELSE ABOARD THE SHIP. I'VE DEVELOPED A BAD HABIT OF TALKING TO MYSELF. I TALK AND TALK AND TALK...
YES.
YOU DO.

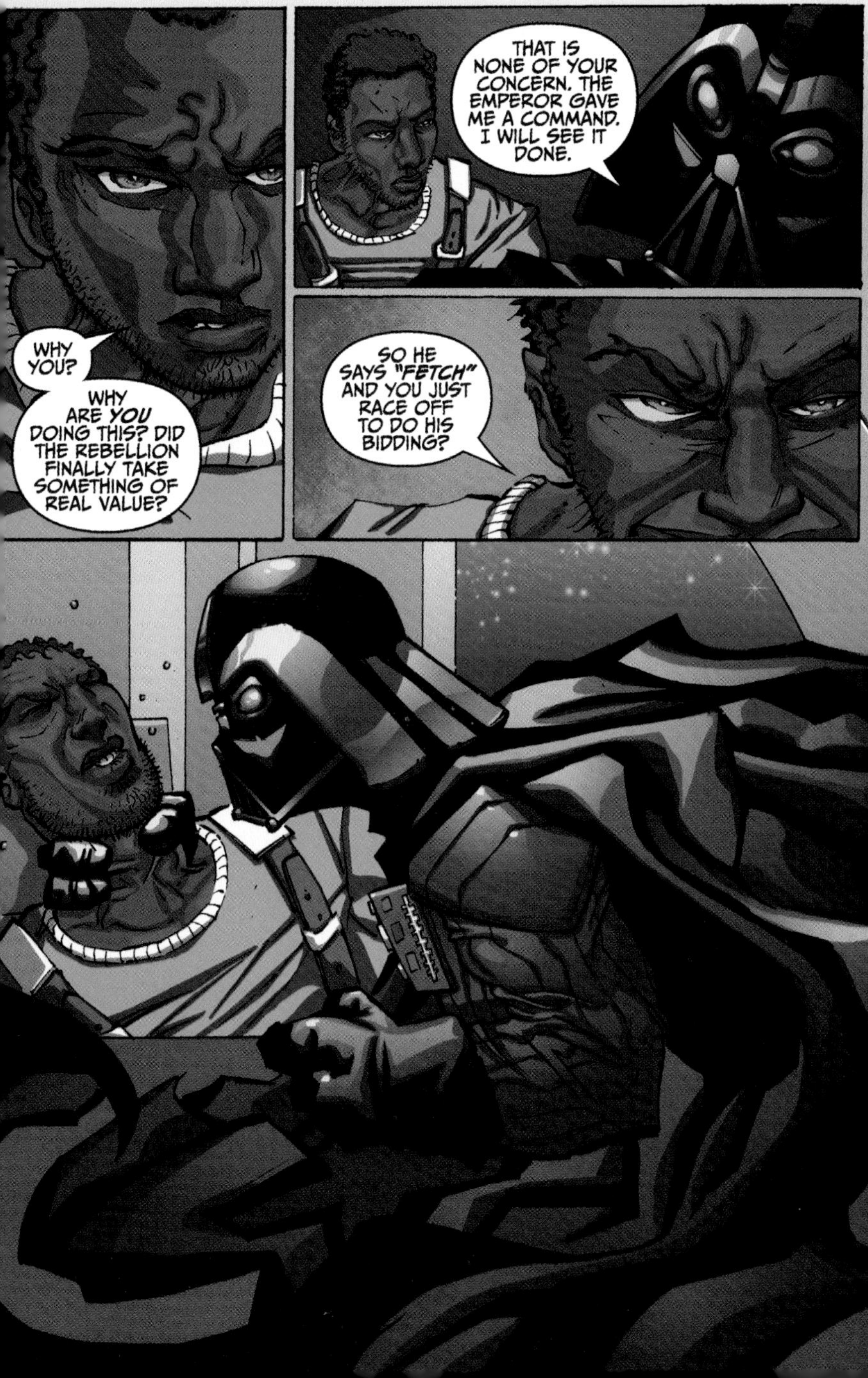
WHY YOU?
WHY ARE YOU DOING THIS? DID THE REBELLION FINALLY TAKE SOMETHING OF REAL VALUE?
THAT IS NONE OF YOUR CONCERN. THE EMPEROR GAVE ME A COMMAND. I WILL SEE IT DONE.
SO HE SAYS "FETCH" AND YOU JUST RACE OFF TO DO HIS BIDDING?

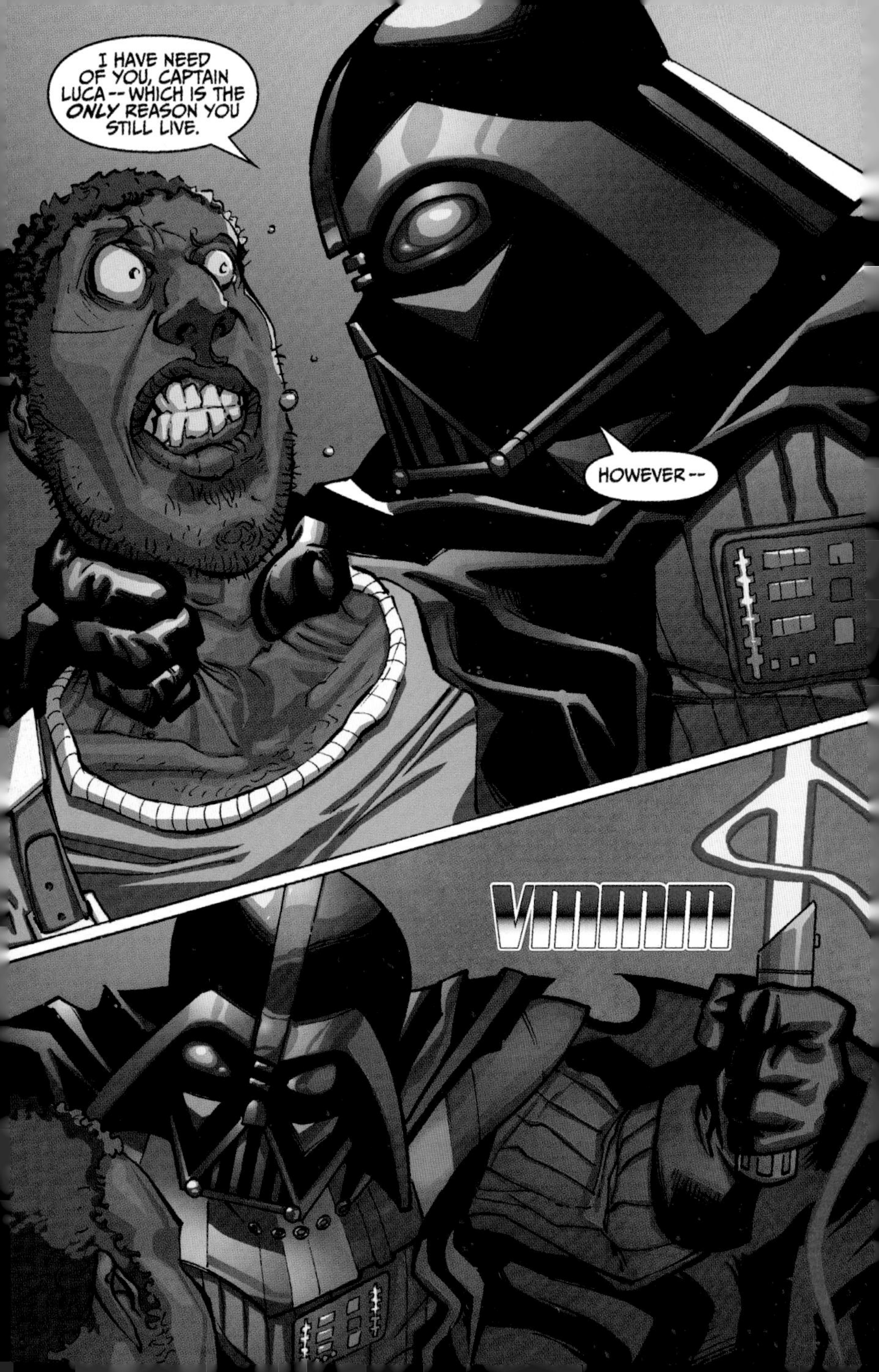

I HAVE NEED OF YOU, CAPTAIN LUCA -- WHICH IS THE *ONLY* REASON YOU STILL LIVE.
HOWEVER --
VMMMM

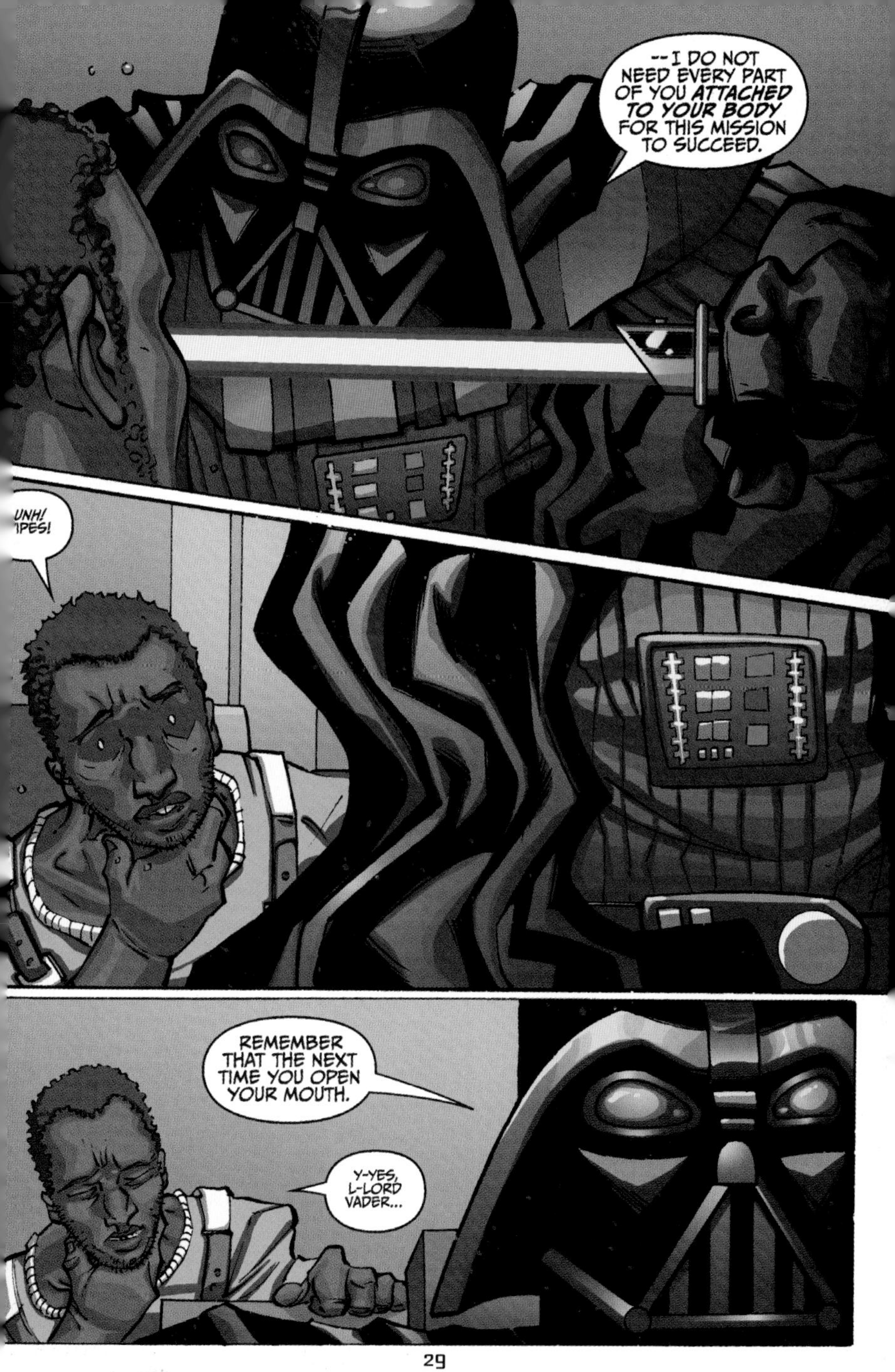
--I DO NOT NEED EVERY PART OF YOU ***ATTACHED TO YOUR BODY*** FOR THIS MISSION TO SUCCEED.
UNH!
PES!
REMEMBER THAT THE NEXT TIME YOU OPEN YOUR MOUTH.
Y-YES, L-LORD VADER...

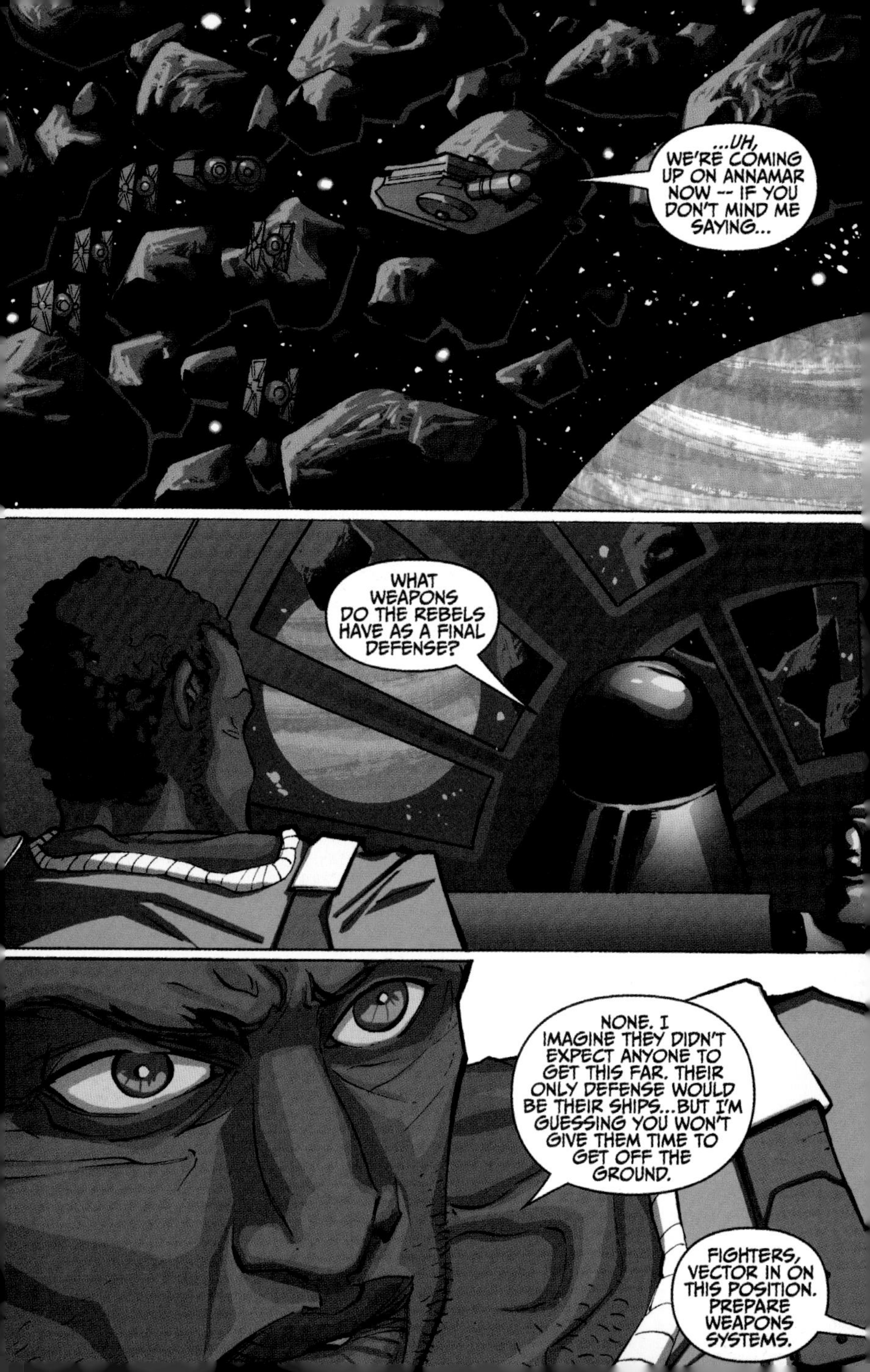
...UH, WE'RE COMING UP ON ANNAMAR NOW -- IF YOU DON'T MIND ME SAYING...
WHAT WEAPONS DO THE REBELS HAVE AS A FINAL DEFENSE?
NONE. I IMAGINE THEY DIDN'T EXPECT ANYONE TO GET THIS FAR. THEIR ONLY DEFENSE WOULD BE THEIR SHIPS...BUT I'M GUESSING YOU WON'T GIVE THEM TIME TO GET OFF THE GROUND.
FIGHTERS, VECTOR IN ON THIS POSITION. PREPARE WEAPONS SYSTEMS.

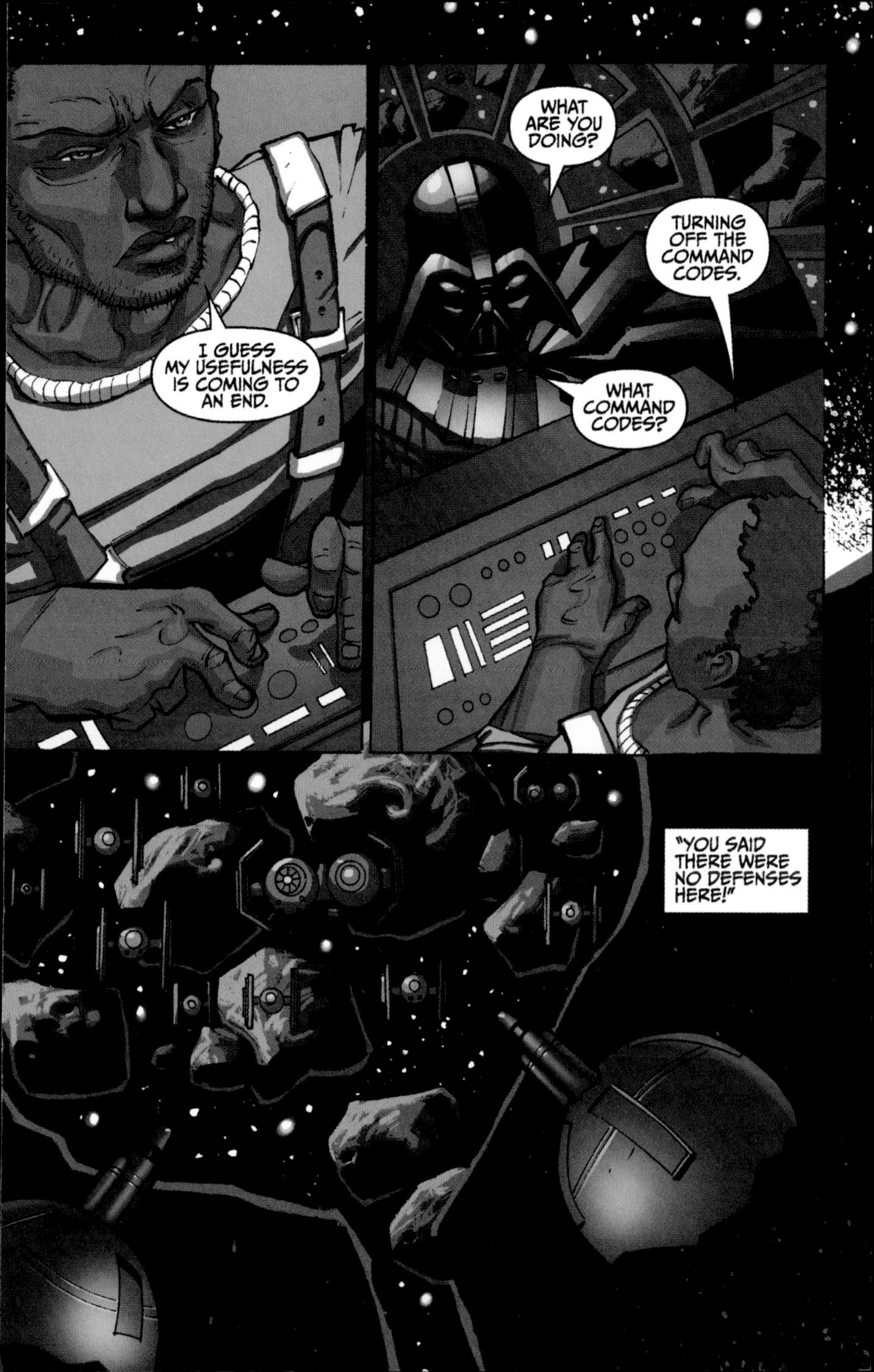
I GUESS MY USEFULNESS IS COMING TO AN END.
WHAT ARE YOU DOING?
TURNING OFF THE COMMAND CODES.
WHAT COMMAND CODES?
"YOU SAID THERE WERE NO DEFENSES HERE!"

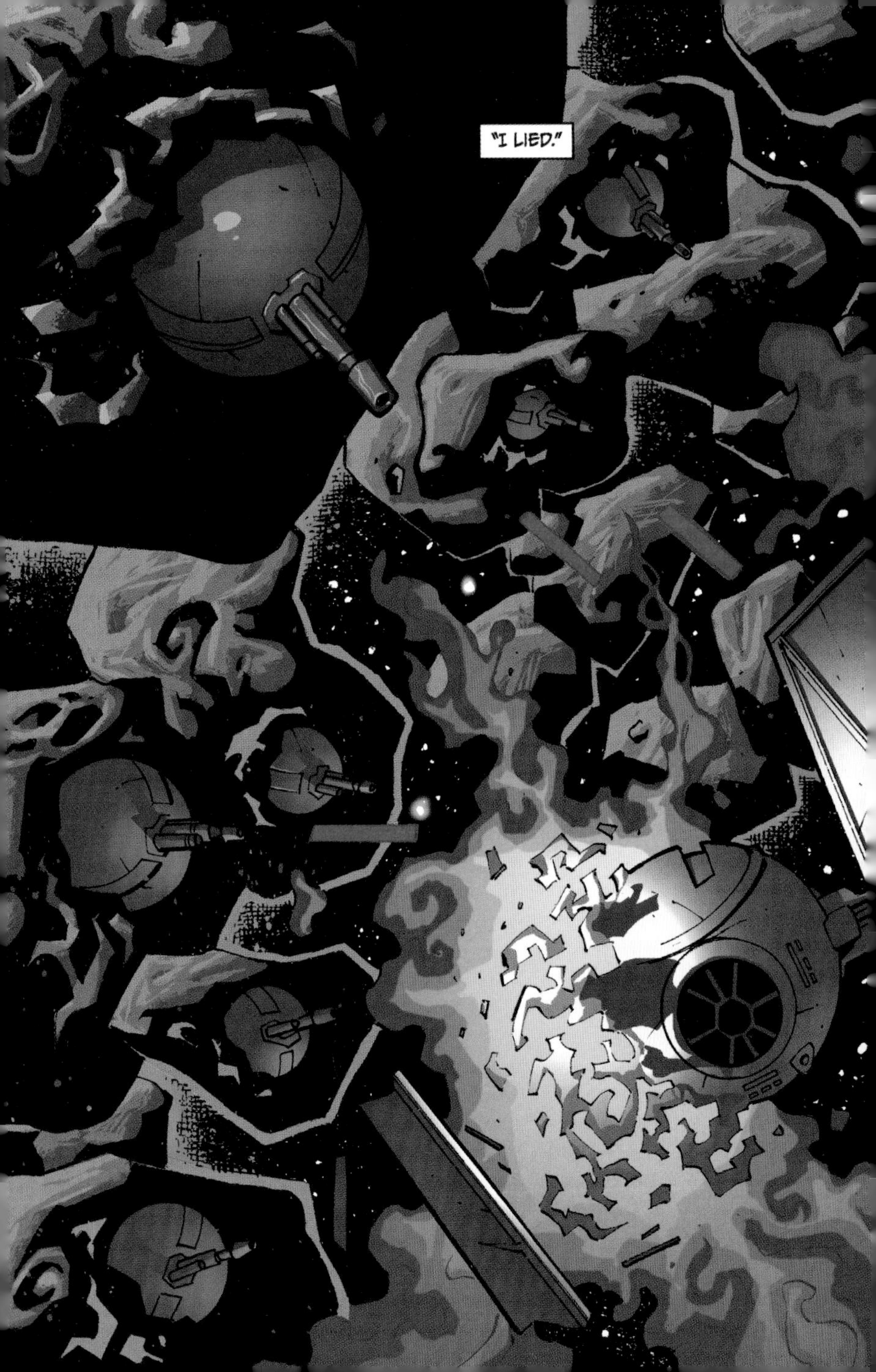
"I LIED."

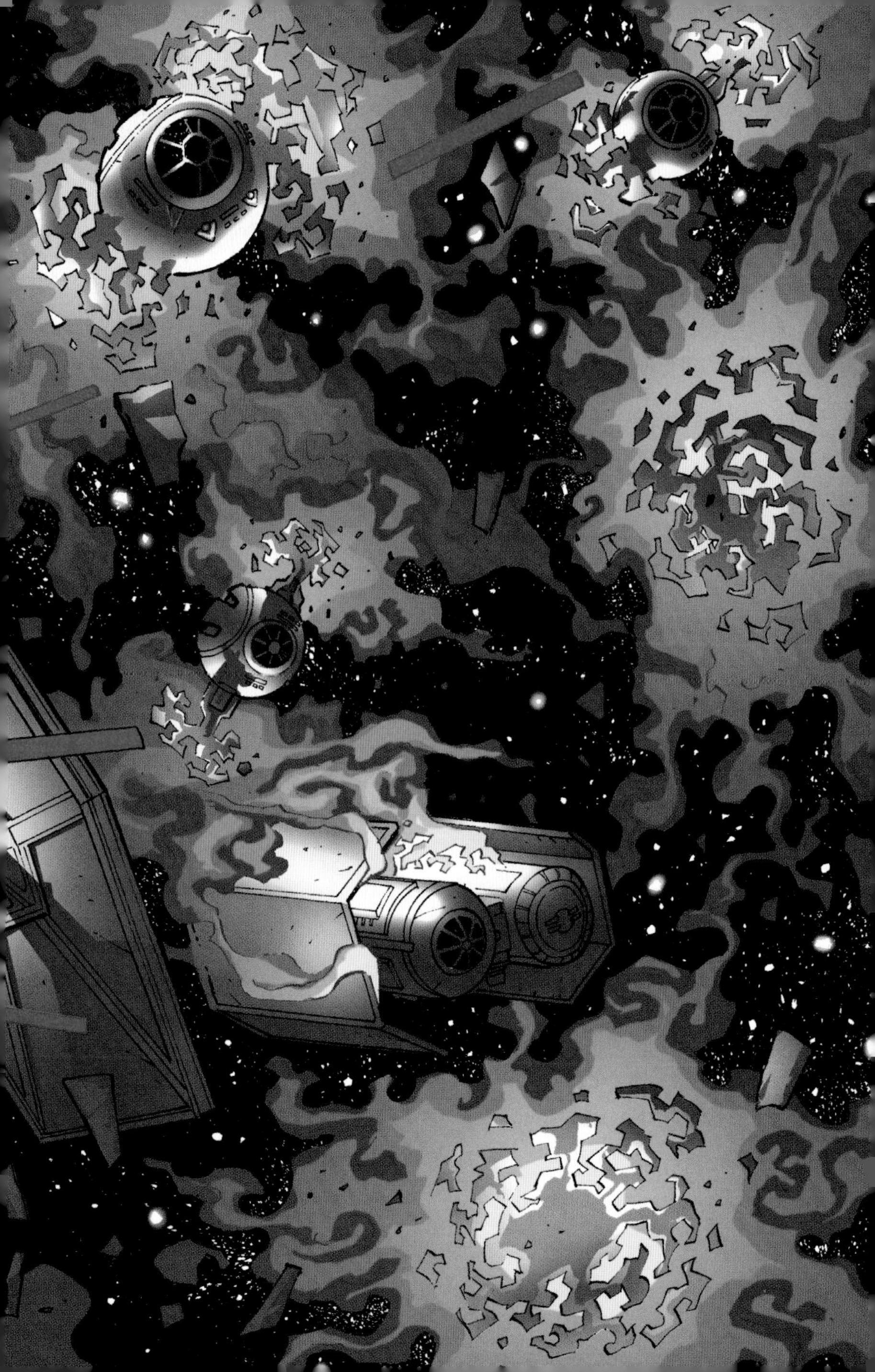

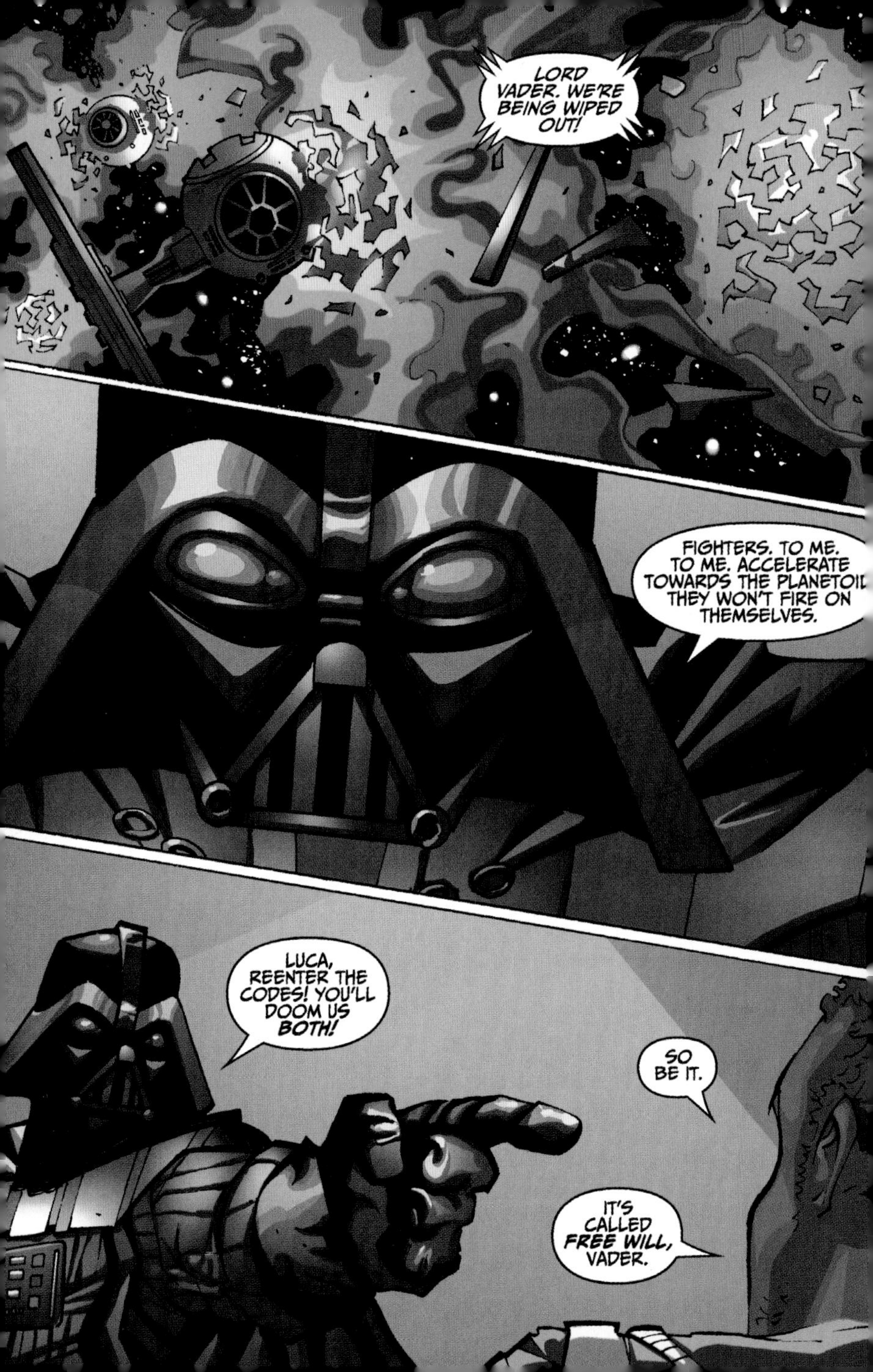
LORD VADER. WE'RE BEING WIPED OUT!
FIGHTERS. TO ME. TO ME. ACCELERATE TOWARDS THE PLANETOID. THEY WON'T FIRE ON THEMSELVES.
LUCA, REENTER THE CODES! YOU'LL DOOM US BOTH!
SO BE IT.
IT'S CALLED FREE WILL, VADER.

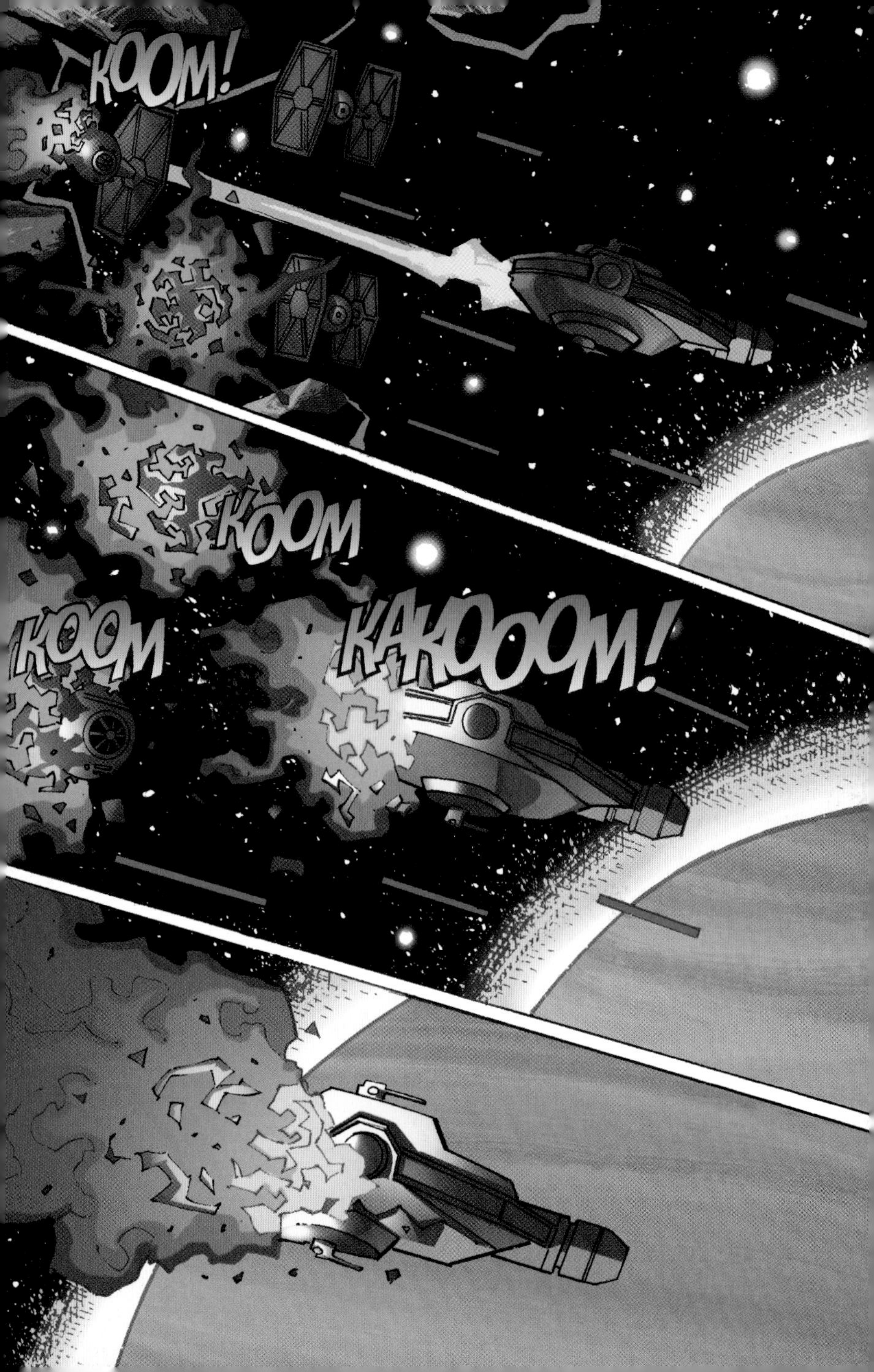
KOOM!
KOOM
KOOM
KAKOOOM!

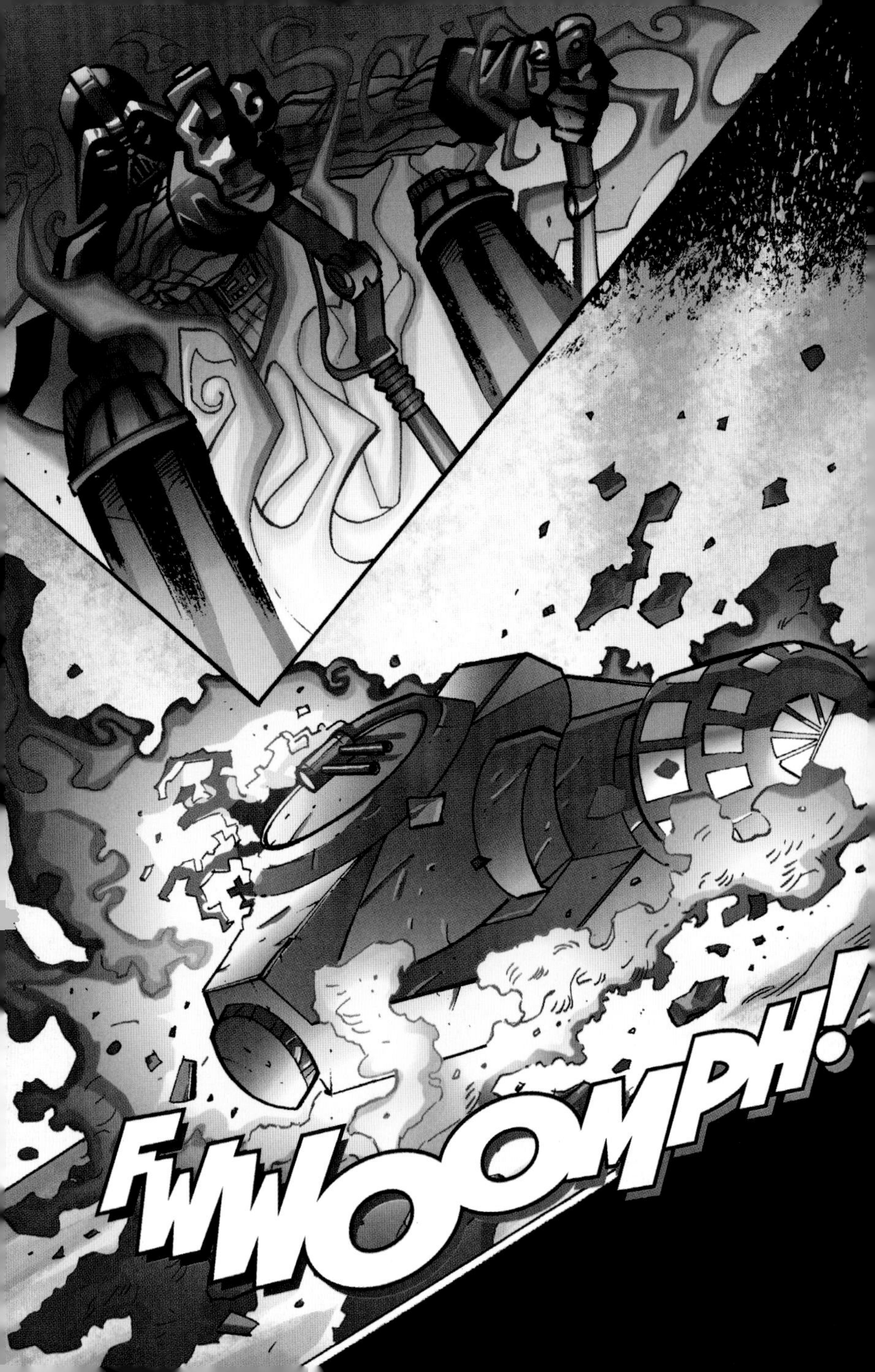
FWWOOOMPH!

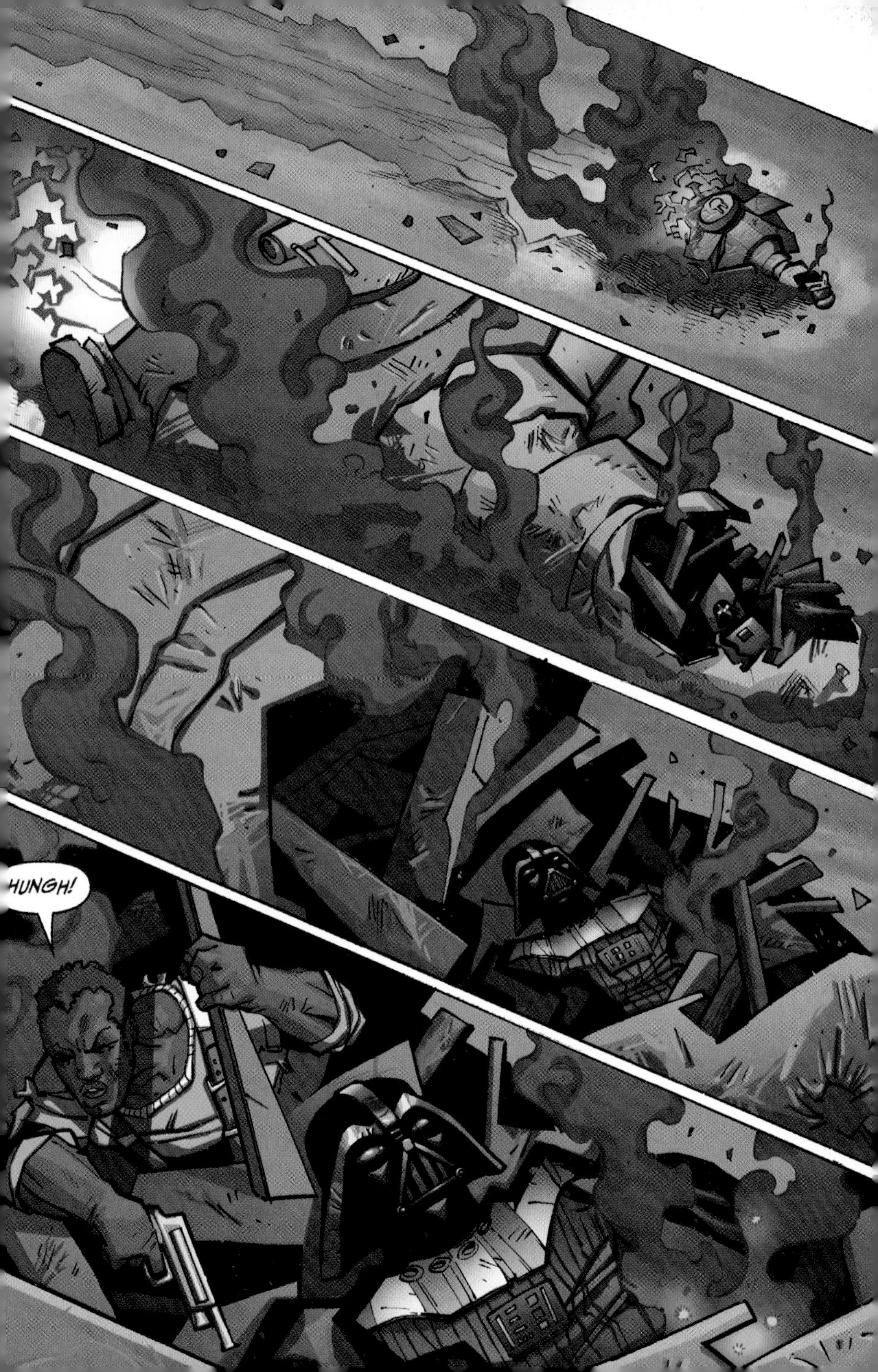
HUNGH!

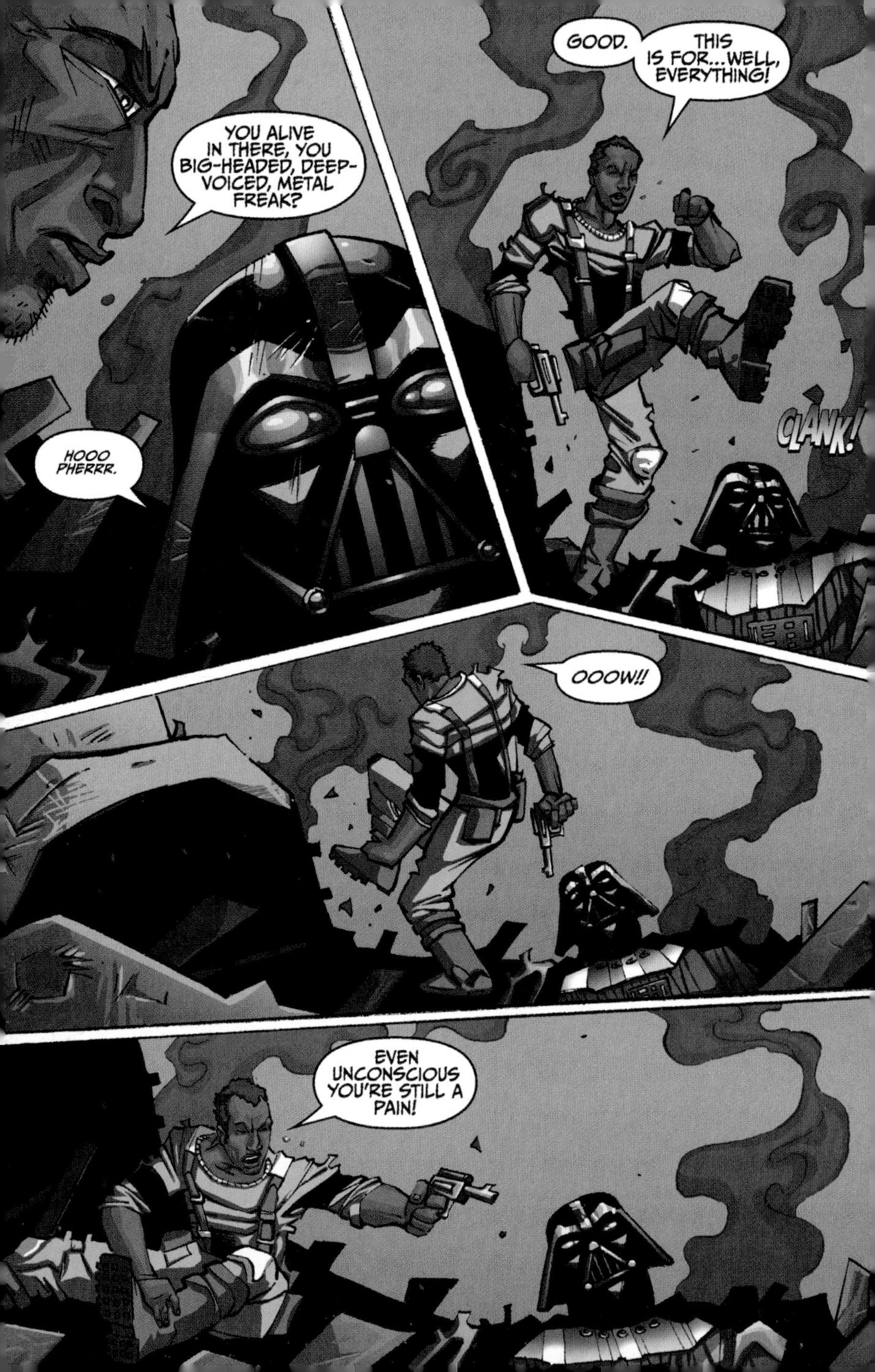
YOU ALIVE IN THERE, YOU BIG-HEADED, DEEP-VOICED, METAL FREAK?
HOOO PHERRR.
GOOD.
THIS IS FOR...WELL, EVERYTHING!
CLANK!
OOOW!!
EVEN UNCONSCIOUS YOU'RE STILL A PAIN!

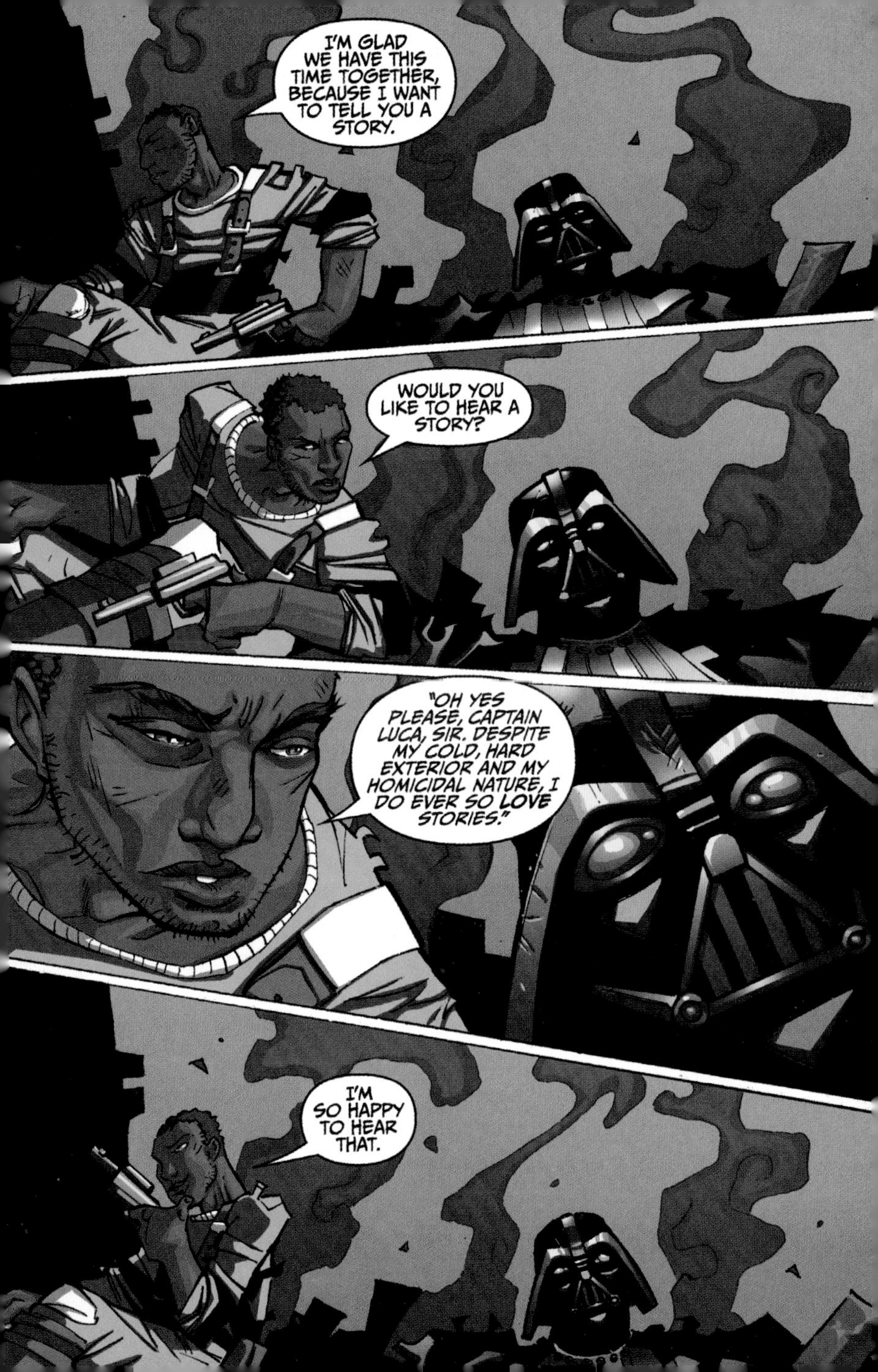
I'M GLAD WE HAVE THIS TIME TOGETHER, BECAUSE I WANT TO TELL YOU A STORY.
WOULD YOU LIKE TO HEAR A STORY?
"OH YES PLEASE, CAPTAIN LUCA, SIR. DESPITE MY COLD, HARD EXTERIOR AND MY HOMICIDAL NATURE, I DO EVER SO LOVE STORIES."
I'M SO HAPPY TO HEAR THAT.

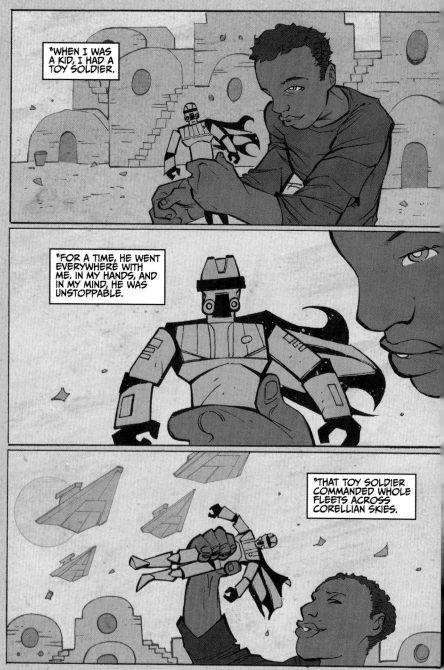

"WHEN I WAS A KID, I HAD A TOY SOLDIER.

"FOR A TIME, HE WENT EVERYWHERE WITH ME. IN MY HANDS, AND IN MY MIND, HE WAS UNSTOPPABLE.

"THAT TOY SOLDIER COMMANDED WHOLE FLEETS ACROSS CORELLIAN SKIES.

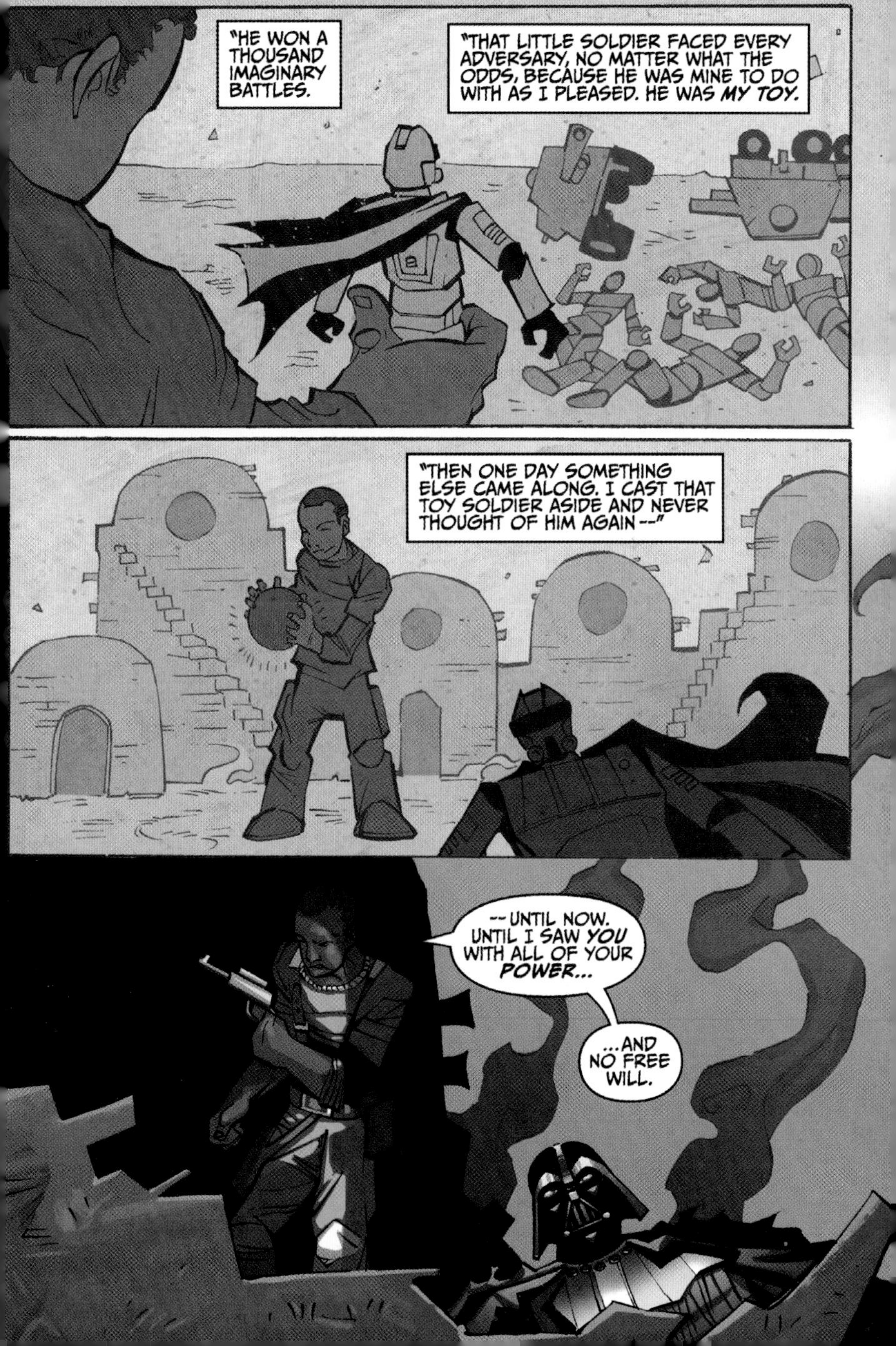
"HE WON A THOUSAND IMAGINARY BATTLES.
"THAT LITTLE SOLDIER FACED EVERY ADVERSARY, NO MATTER WHAT THE ODDS, BECAUSE HE WAS MINE TO DO WITH AS I PLEASED. HE WAS MY TOY.
"THEN ONE DAY SOMETHING ELSE CAME ALONG. I CAST THAT TOY SOLDIER ASIDE AND NEVER THOUGHT OF HIM AGAIN--"
--UNTIL NOW. UNTIL I SAW YOU WITH ALL OF YOUR POWER...
...AND NO FREE WILL.

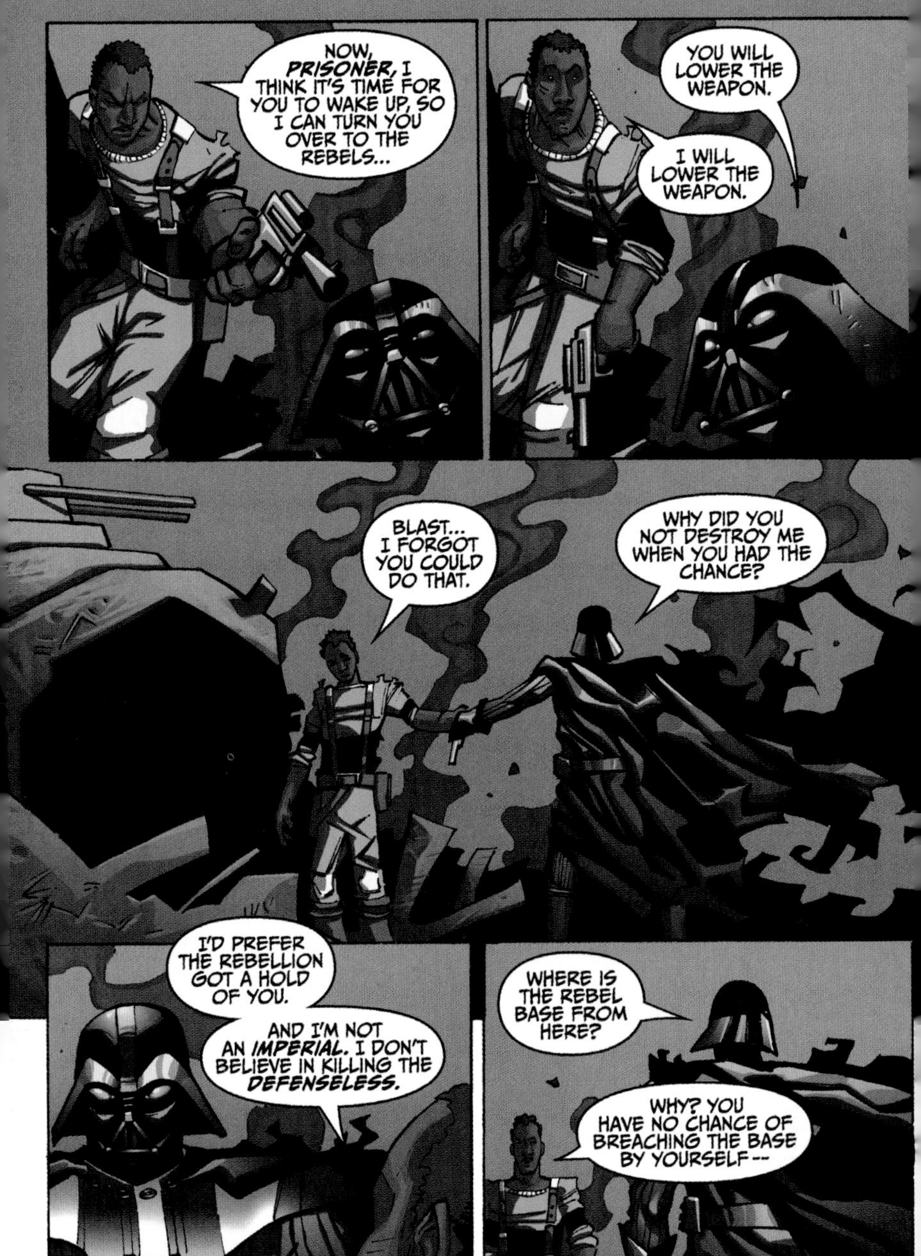

NOW, *PRISONER,* I THINK IT'S TIME FOR YOU TO WAKE UP, SO I CAN TURN YOU OVER TO THE REBELS...
YOU WILL LOWER THE WEAPON.
I WILL LOWER THE WEAPON.
BLAST... I FORGOT YOU COULD DO THAT.
WHY DID YOU NOT DESTROY ME WHEN YOU HAD THE CHANCE?
I'D PREFER THE REBELLION GOT A HOLD OF YOU.
AND I'M NOT AN *IMPERIAL.* I DON'T BELIEVE IN KILLING THE *DEFENSELESS.*
WHERE IS THE REBEL BASE FROM HERE?
WHY? YOU HAVE NO CHANCE OF BREACHING THE BASE BY YOURSELF--

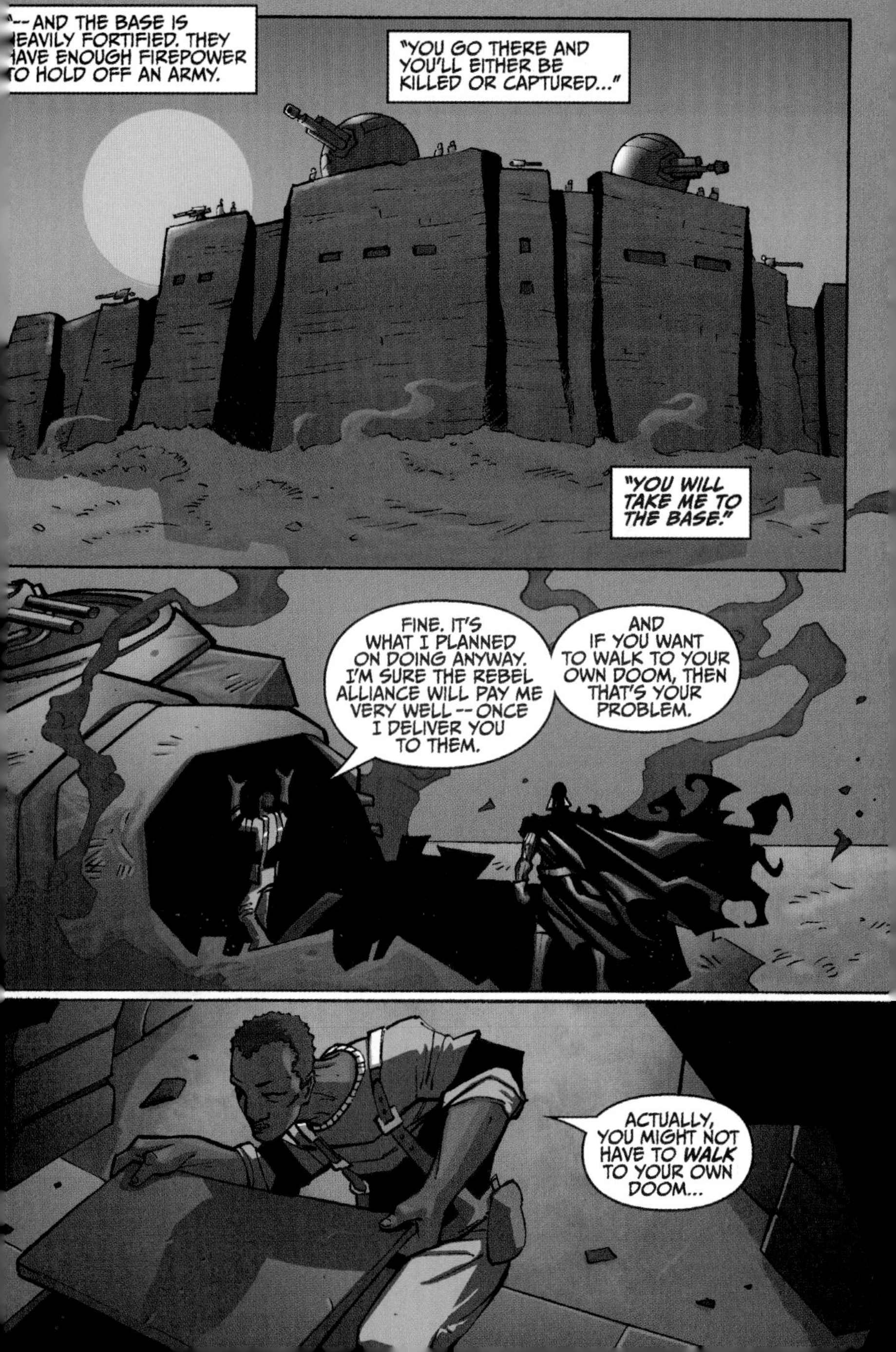
"--AND THE BASE IS HEAVILY FORTIFIED. THEY HAVE ENOUGH FIREPOWER TO HOLD OFF AN ARMY.
"YOU GO THERE AND YOU'LL EITHER BE KILLED OR CAPTURED..."
"YOU WILL TAKE ME TO THE BASE."
FINE. IT'S WHAT I PLANNED ON DOING ANYWAY. I'M SURE THE REBEL ALLIANCE WILL PAY ME VERY WELL--ONCE I DELIVER YOU TO THEM.
AND IF YOU WANT TO WALK TO YOUR OWN DOOM, THEN THAT'S YOUR PROBLEM.
ACTUALLY, YOU MIGHT NOT HAVE TO WALK TO YOUR OWN DOOM...

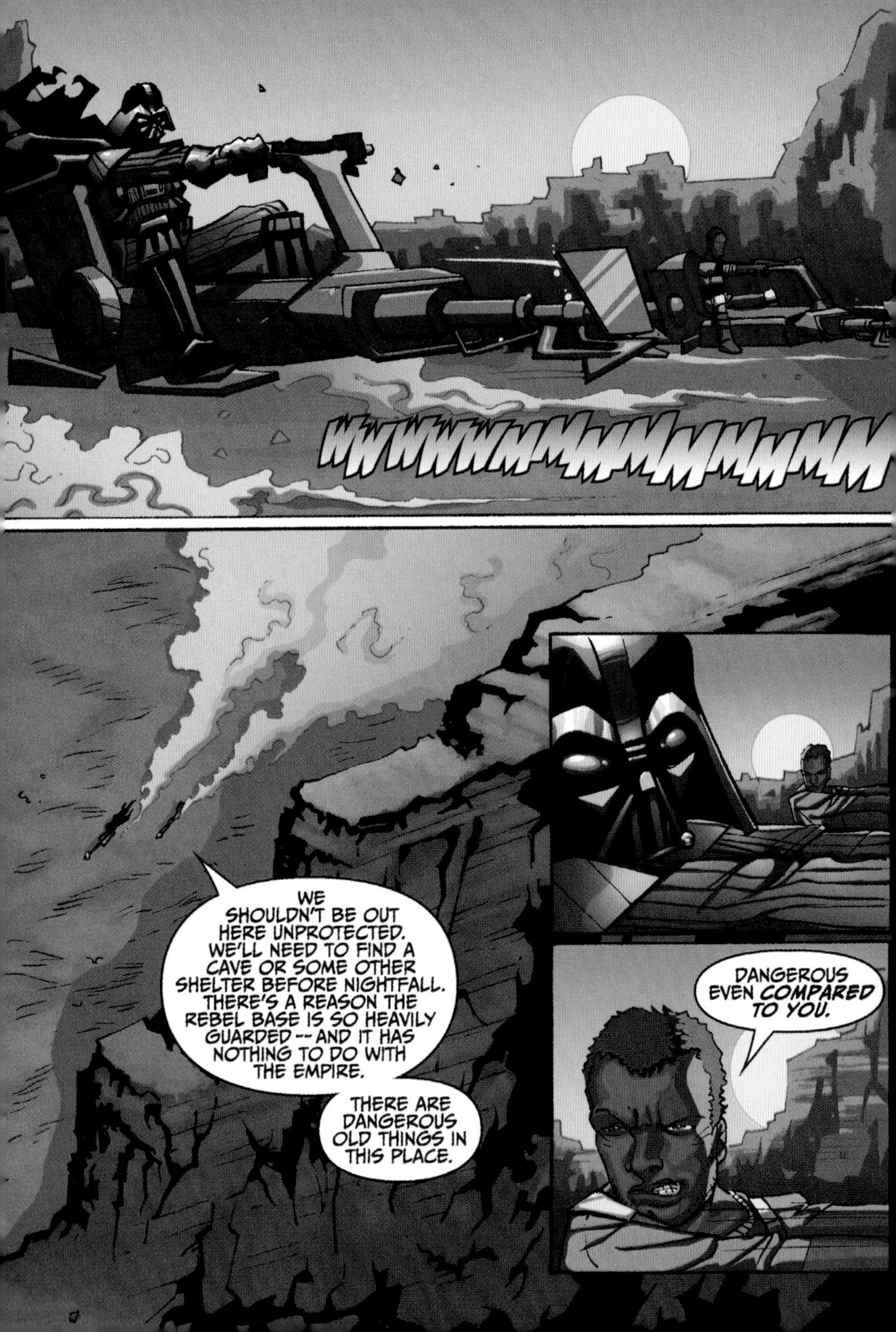
WWWWWMMMMMMMMMMMM
WE SHOULDN'T BE OUT HERE UNPROTECTED. WE'LL NEED TO FIND A CAVE OR SOME OTHER SHELTER BEFORE NIGHTFALL. THERE'S A REASON THE REBEL BASE IS SO HEAVILY GUARDED-- AND IT HAS NOTHING TO DO WITH THE EMPIRE.
THERE ARE DANGEROUS OLD THINGS IN THIS PLACE.
DANGEROUS EVEN COMPARED TO YOU.

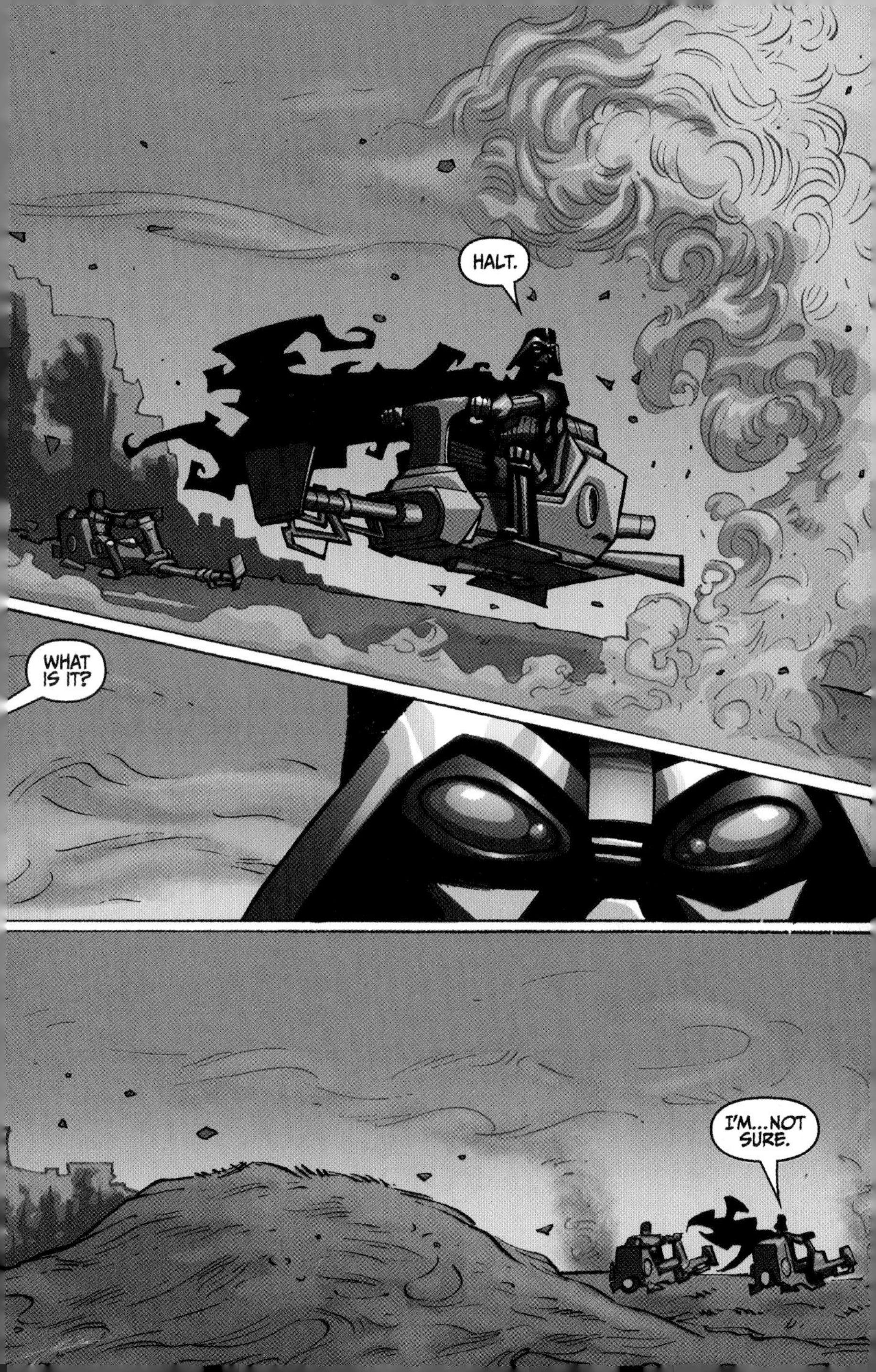
HALT.
WHAT IS IT?
I'M...NOT SURE.

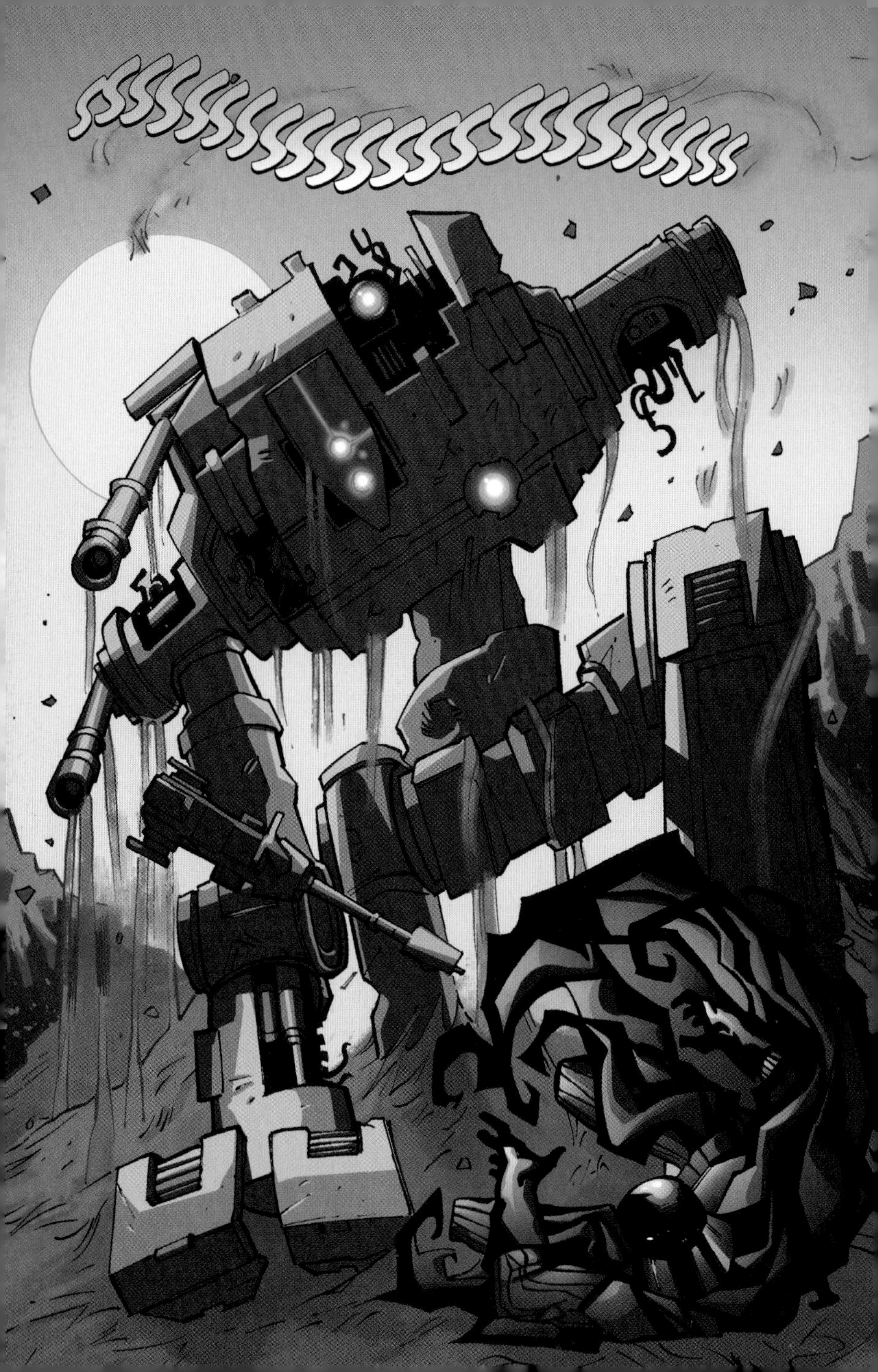
SSSSSSSSSSSSSSSSSSSSSSS

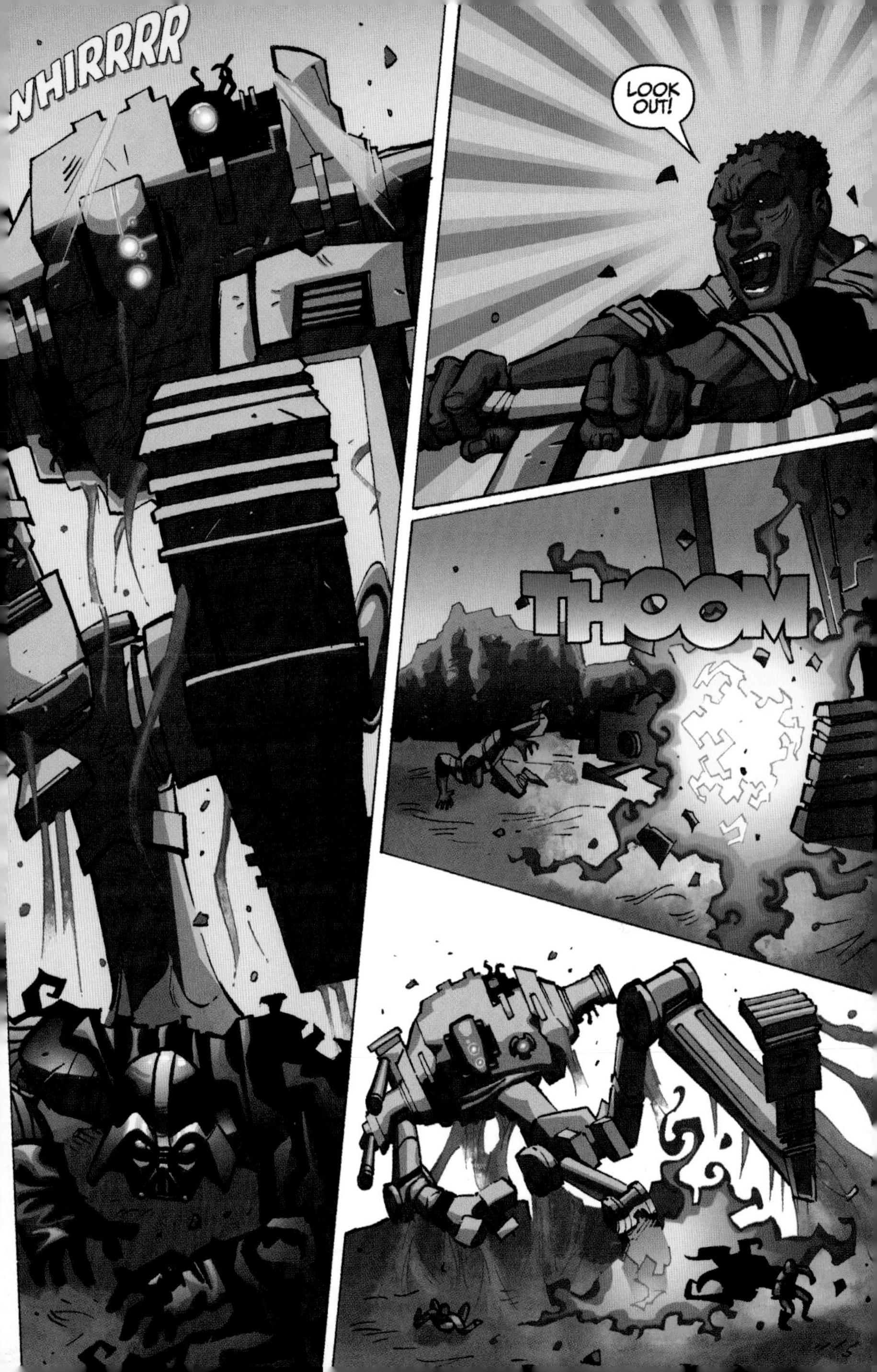
WHIRRRR
LOOK OUT!
THOOM

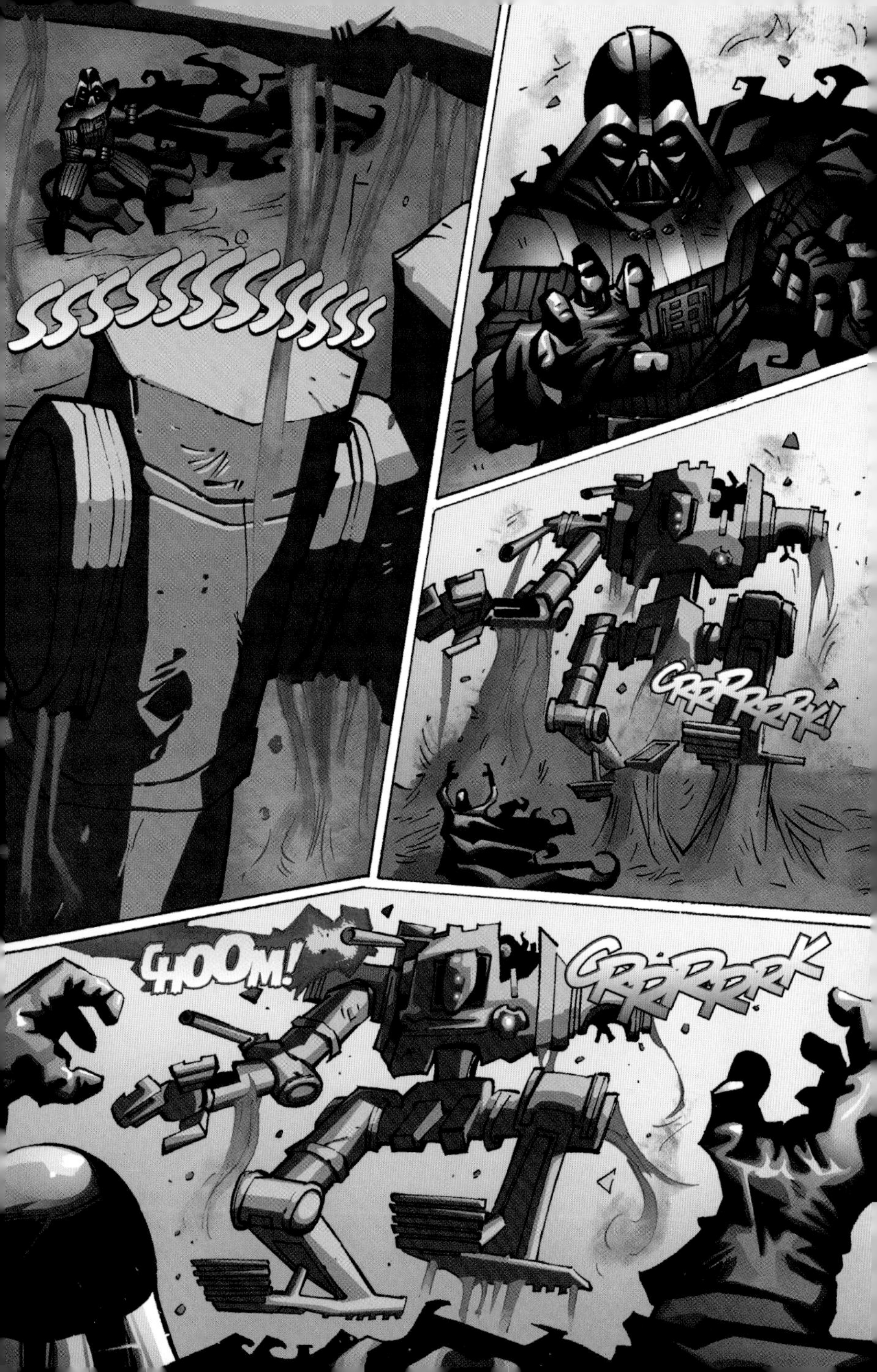
SSSSSSSSSSSSSS
GRRRRRRK!
CHOOM!
GRRRRRRK

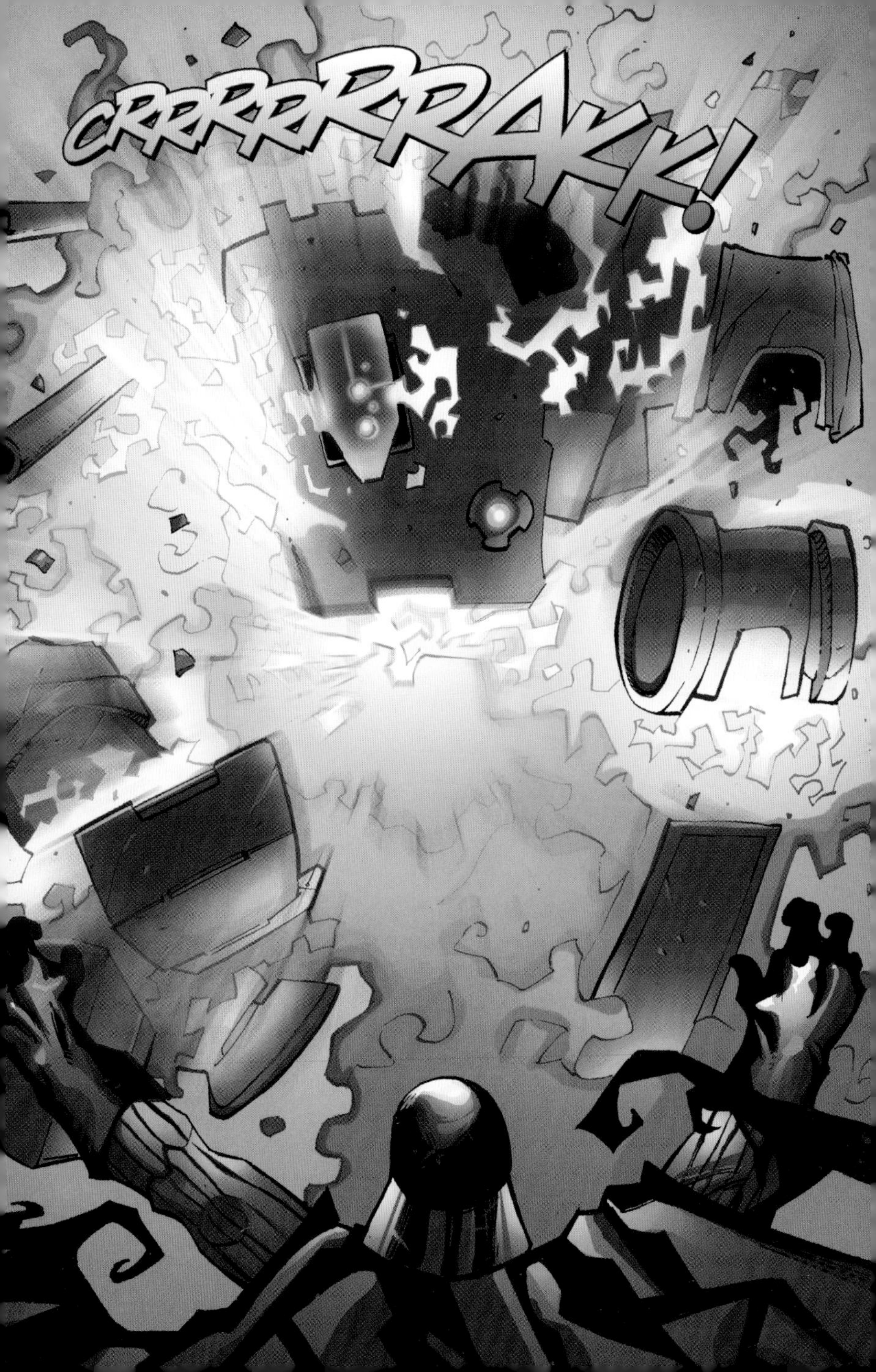
CRRRRRRAKK!

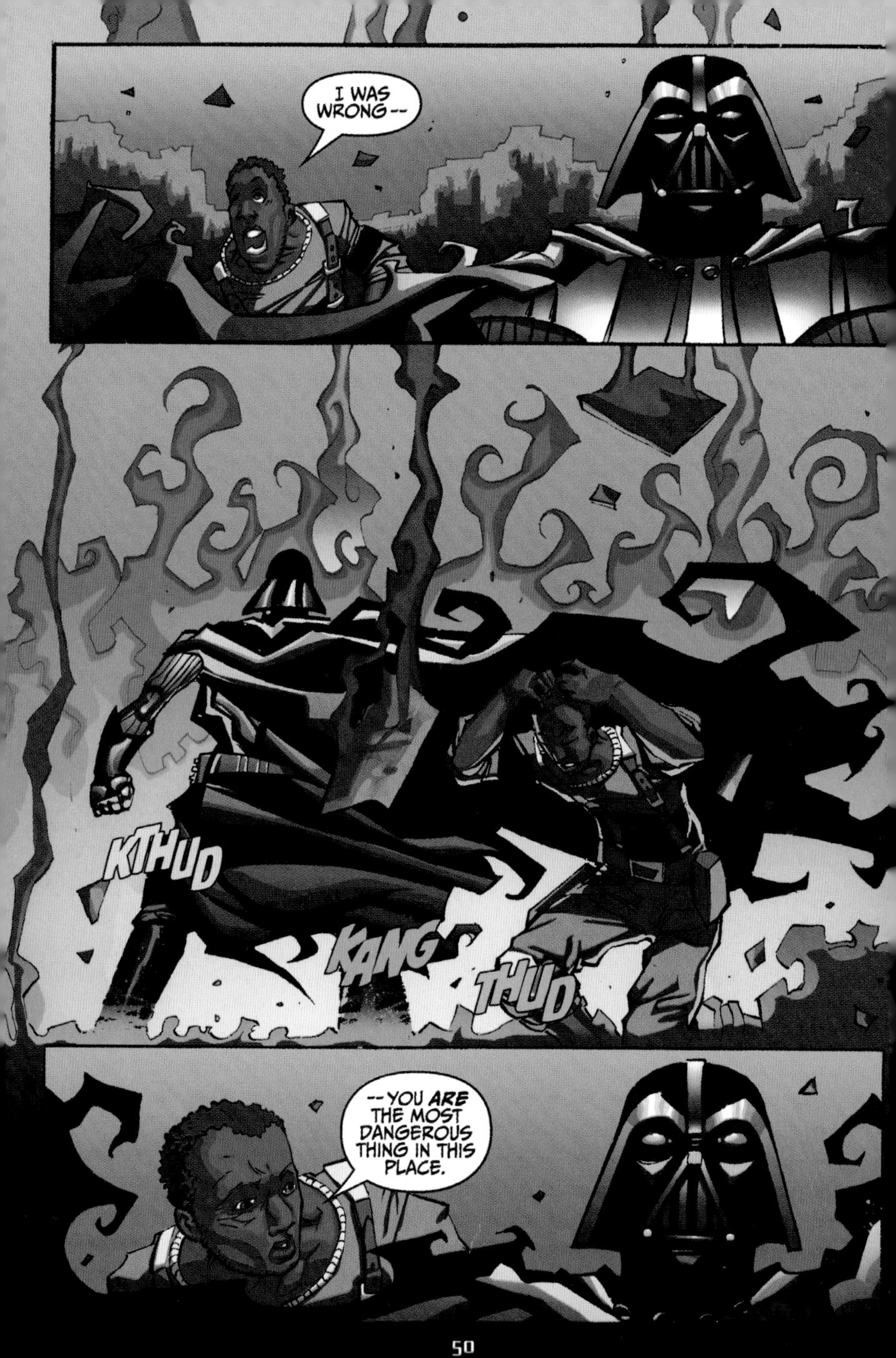
I WAS WRONG--
KTHUD
KANG
THUD
--YOU ARE THE MOST DANGEROUS THING IN THIS PLACE.

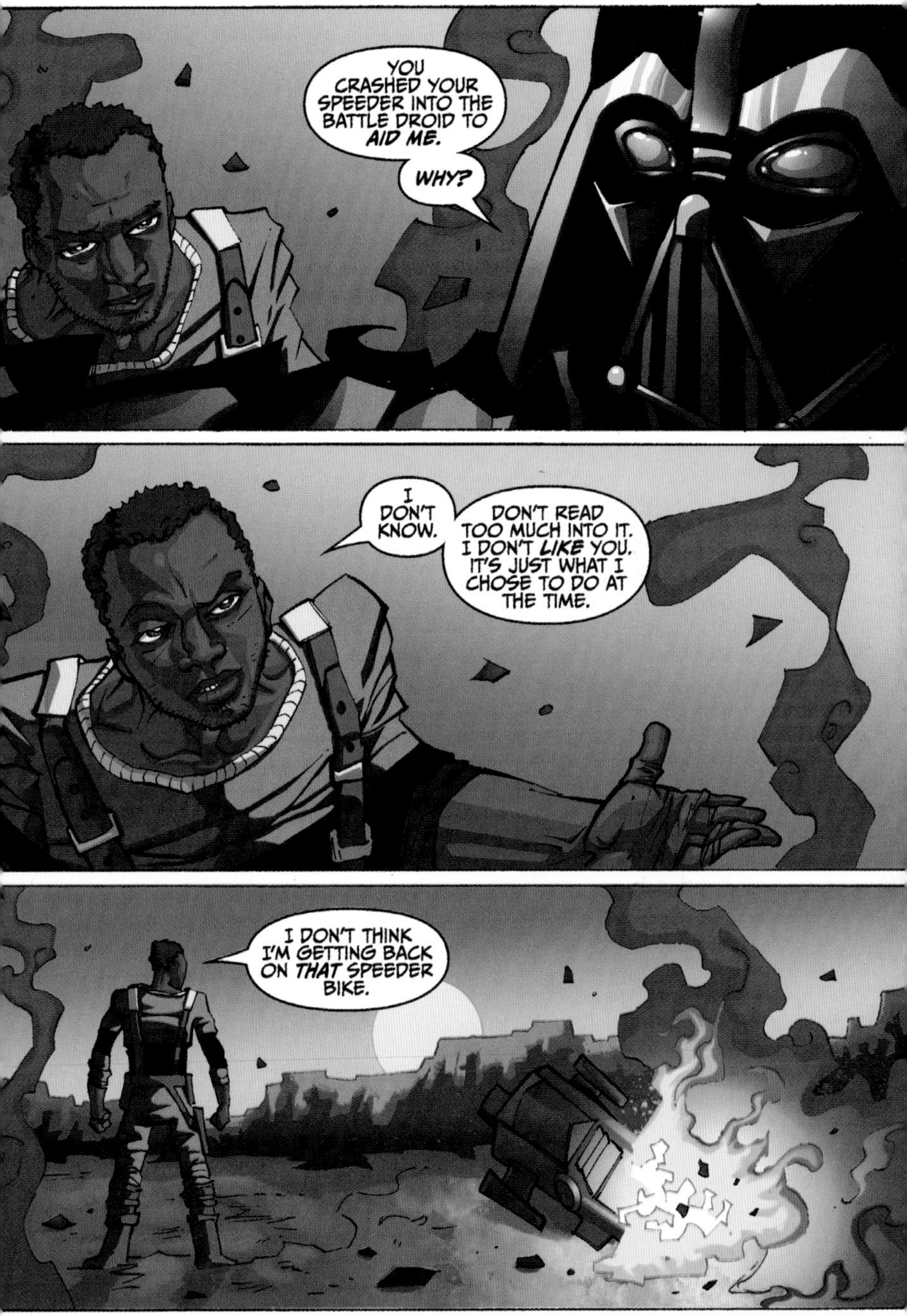
YOU CRASHED YOUR SPEEDER INTO THE BATTLE DROID TO *AID ME.*
WHY?
I DON'T KNOW.
DON'T READ TOO MUCH INTO IT. I DON'T *LIKE* YOU. IT'S JUST WHAT I CHOSE TO DO AT THE TIME.
I DON'T THINK I'M GETTING BACK ON *THAT* SPEEDER BIKE.

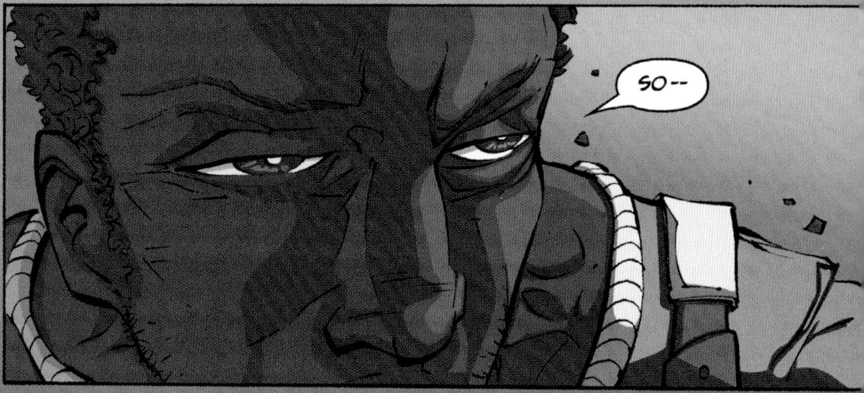
SO--

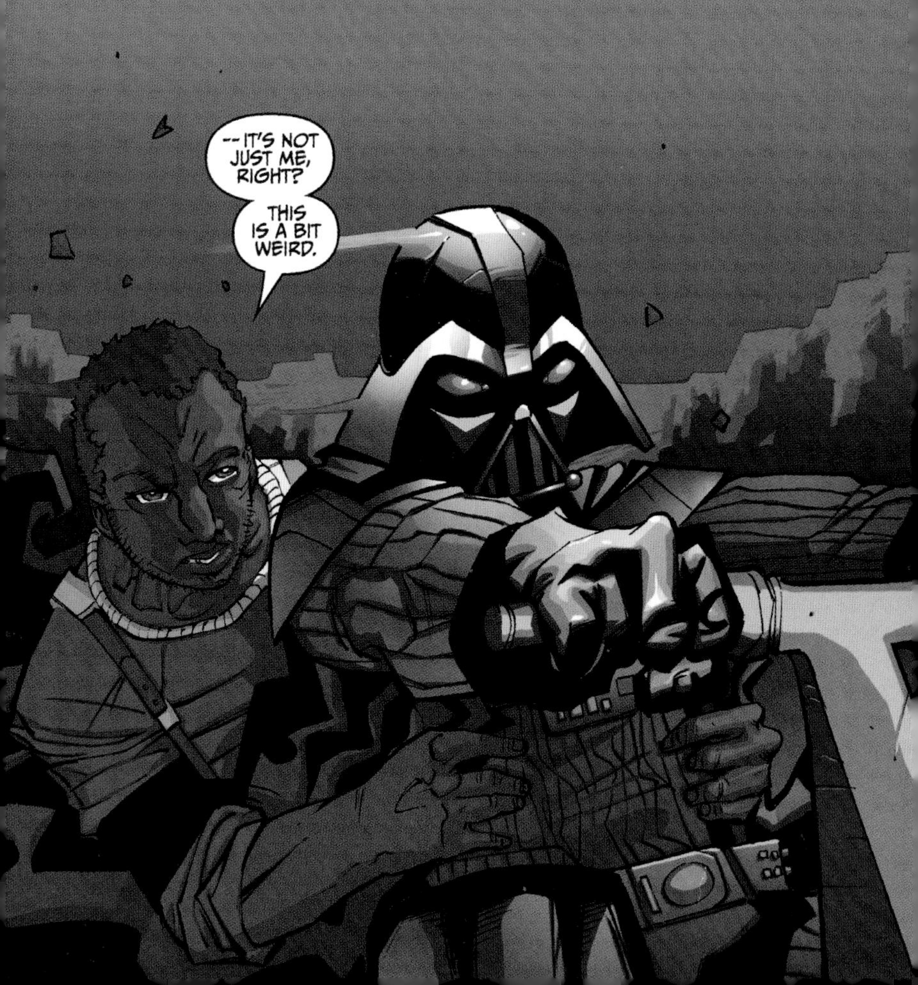
--IT'S NOT JUST ME, RIGHT?
THIS IS A BIT WEIRD.

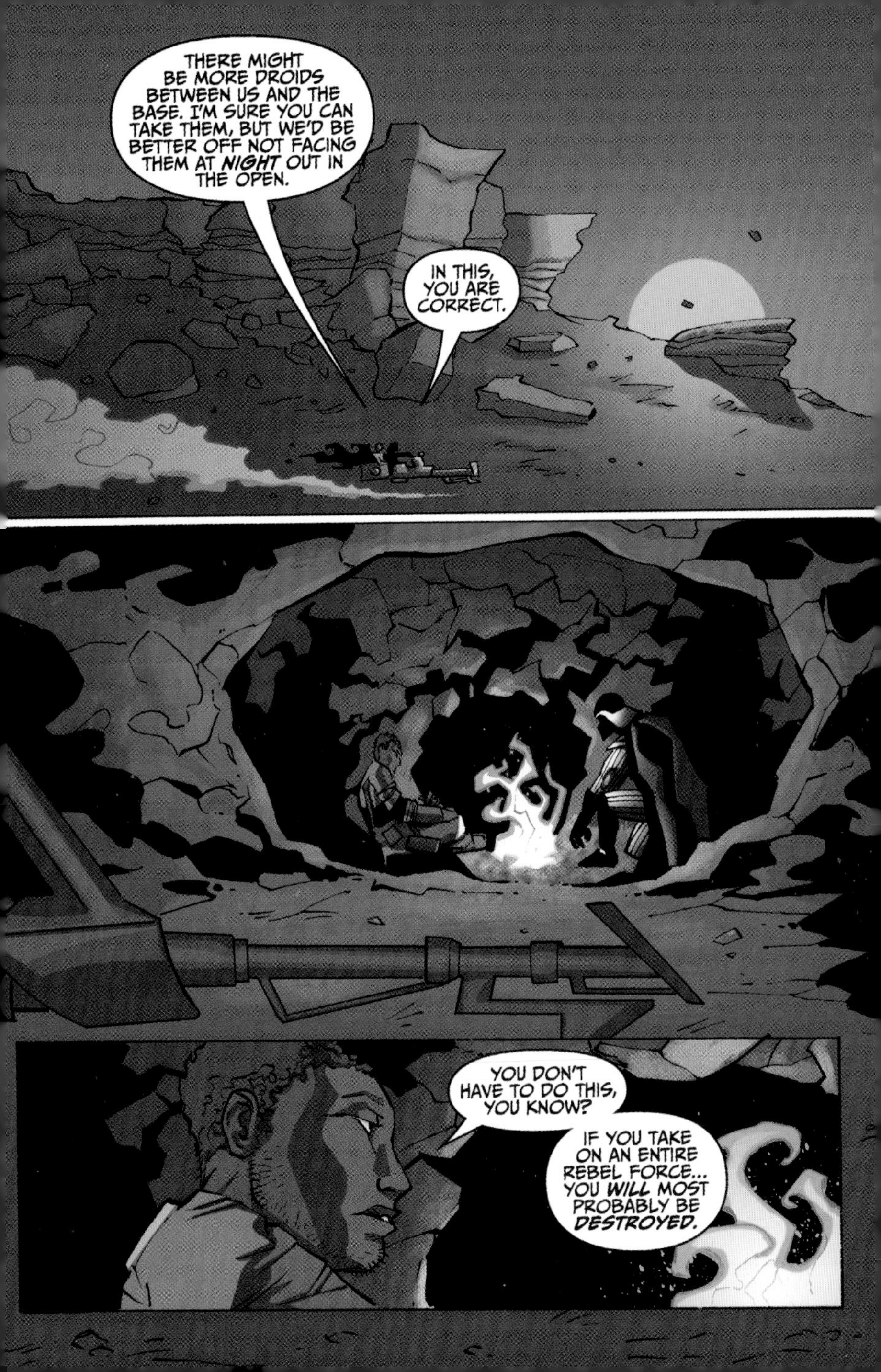
THERE MIGHT BE MORE DROIDS BETWEEN US AND THE BASE. I'M SURE YOU CAN TAKE THEM, BUT WE'D BE BETTER OFF NOT FACING THEM AT NIGHT OUT IN THE OPEN.
IN THIS, YOU ARE CORRECT.
YOU DON'T HAVE TO DO THIS, YOU KNOW?
IF YOU TAKE ON AN ENTIRE REBEL FORCE... YOU WILL MOST PROBABLY BE DESTROYED.

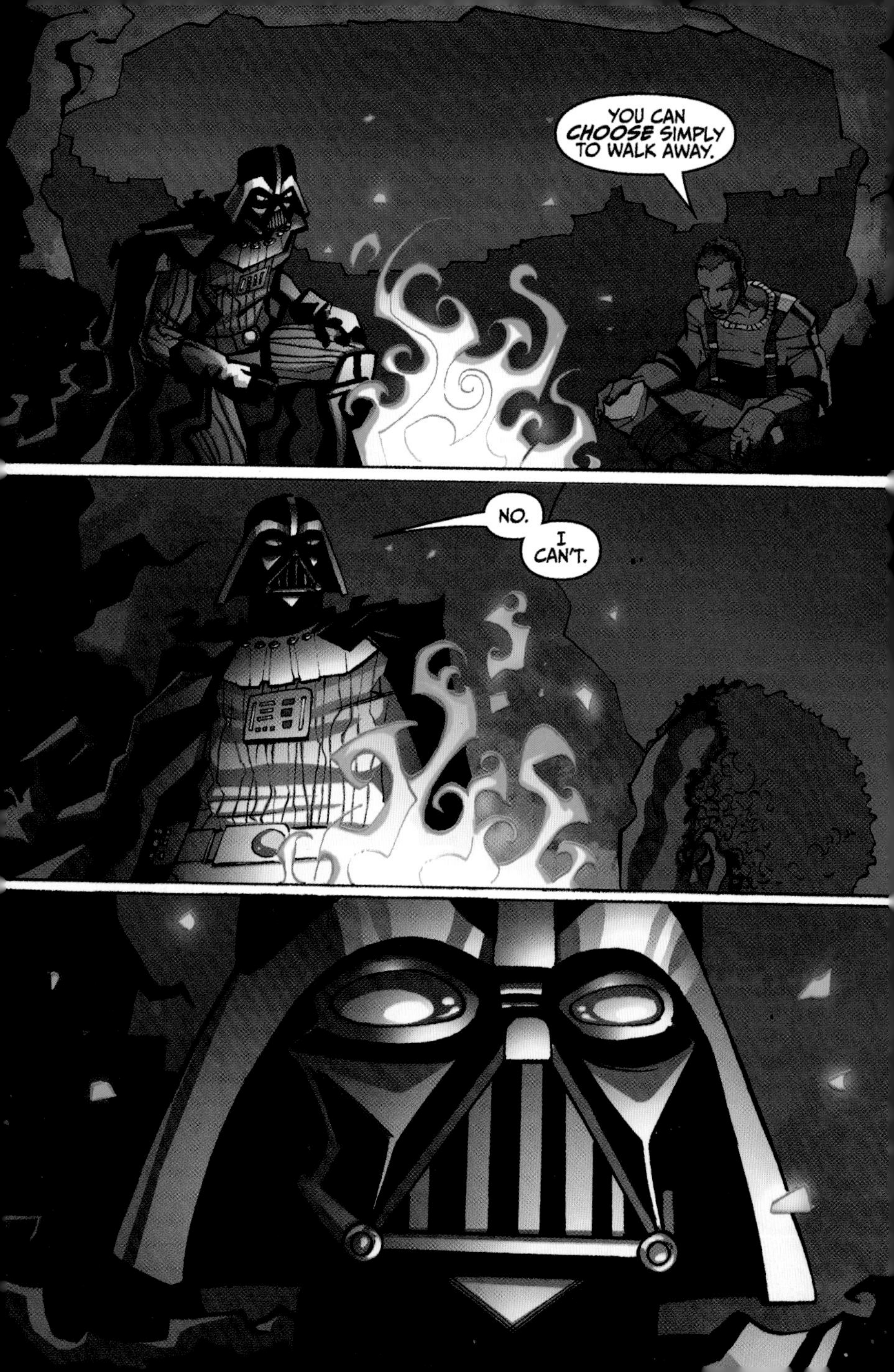
YOU CAN *CHOOSE* SIMPLY TO WALK AWAY.
NO.
I CAN'T.

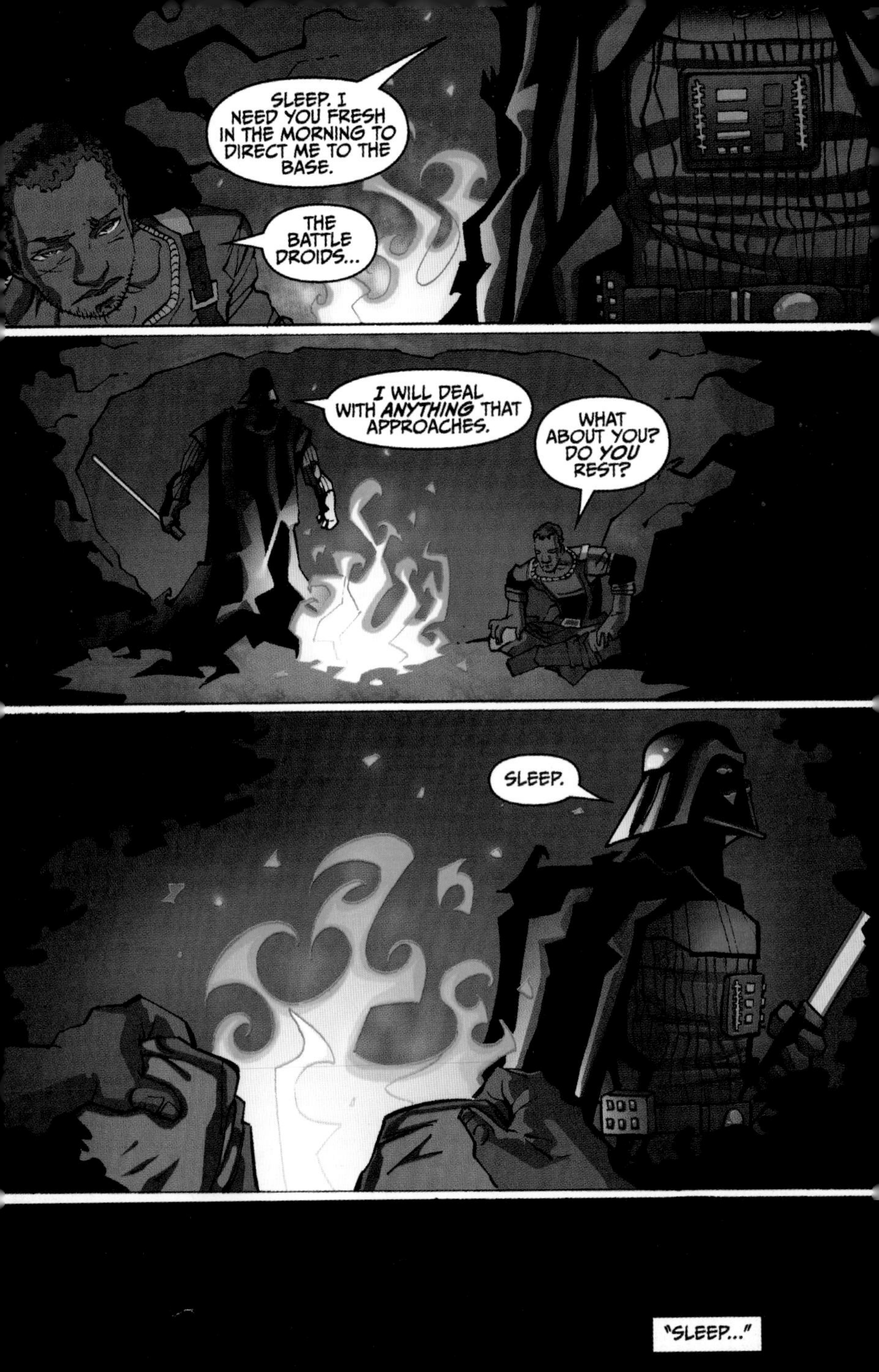
SLEEP. I NEED YOU FRESH IN THE MORNING TO DIRECT ME TO THE BASE.
THE BATTLE DROIDS...
I WILL DEAL WITH ANYTHING THAT APPROACHES.
WHAT ABOUT YOU? DO YOU REST?
SLEEP.
"SLEEP..."

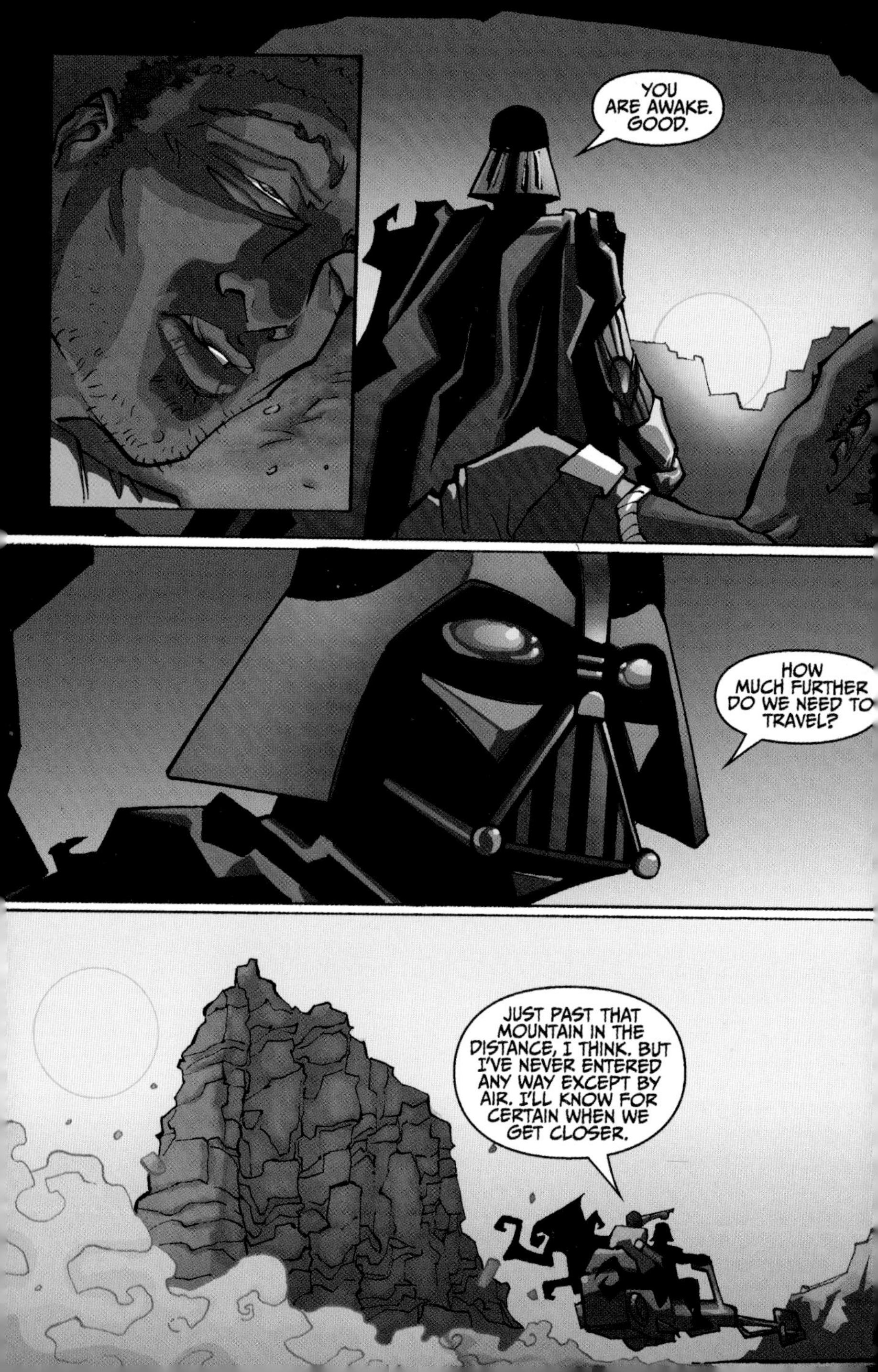
YOU ARE AWAKE. GOOD.
HOW MUCH FURTHER DO WE NEED TO TRAVEL?
JUST PAST THAT MOUNTAIN IN THE DISTANCE, I THINK. BUT I'VE NEVER ENTERED ANY WAY EXCEPT BY AIR. I'LL KNOW FOR CERTAIN WHEN WE GET CLOSER.

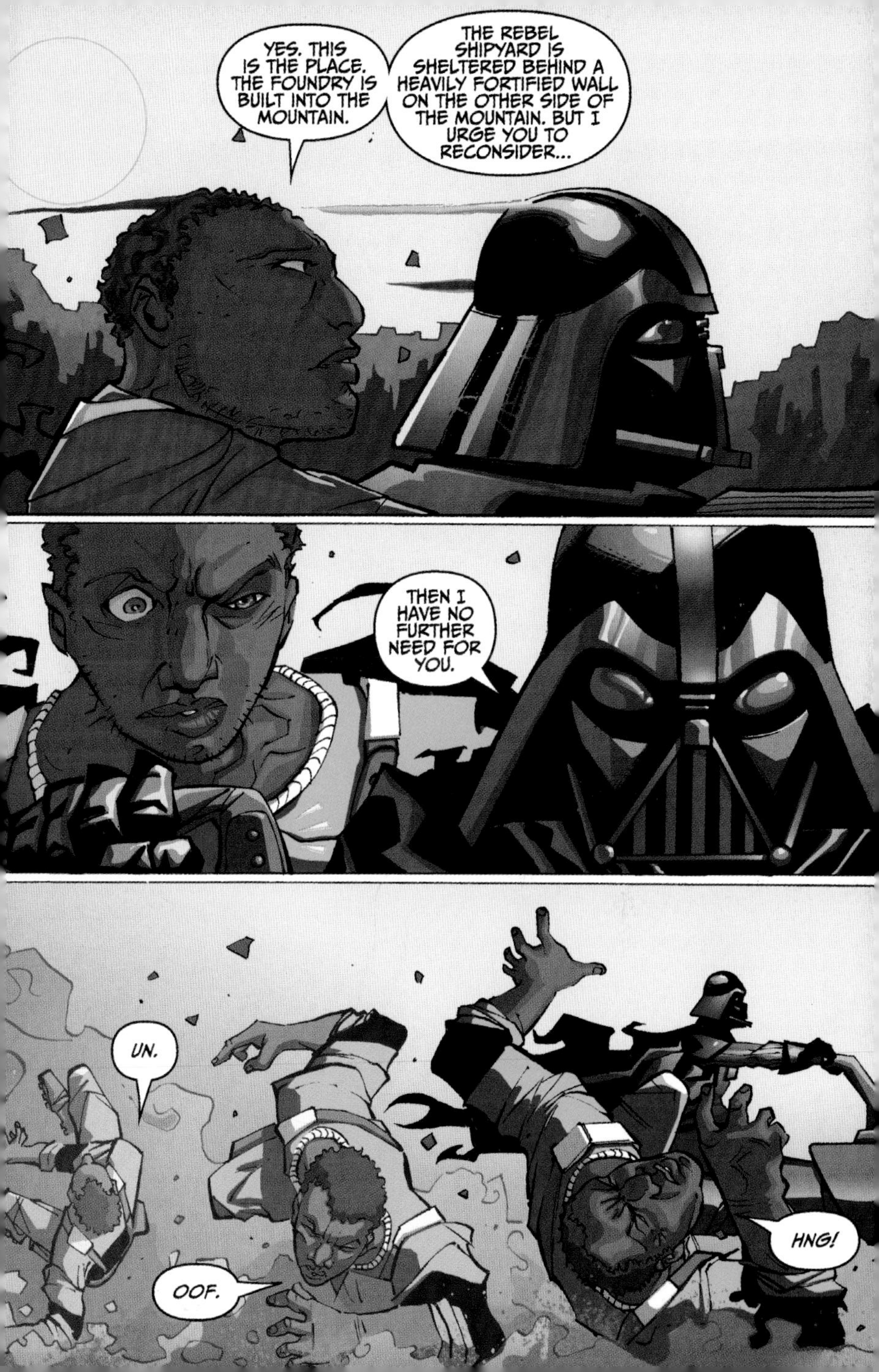
YES. THIS IS THE PLACE. THE FOUNDRY IS BUILT INTO THE MOUNTAIN.
THE REBEL SHIPYARD IS SHELTERED BEHIND A HEAVILY FORTIFIED WALL ON THE OTHER SIDE OF THE MOUNTAIN. BUT I URGE YOU TO RECONSIDER...
THEN I HAVE NO FURTHER NEED FOR YOU.
UN.
OOF.
HNG!

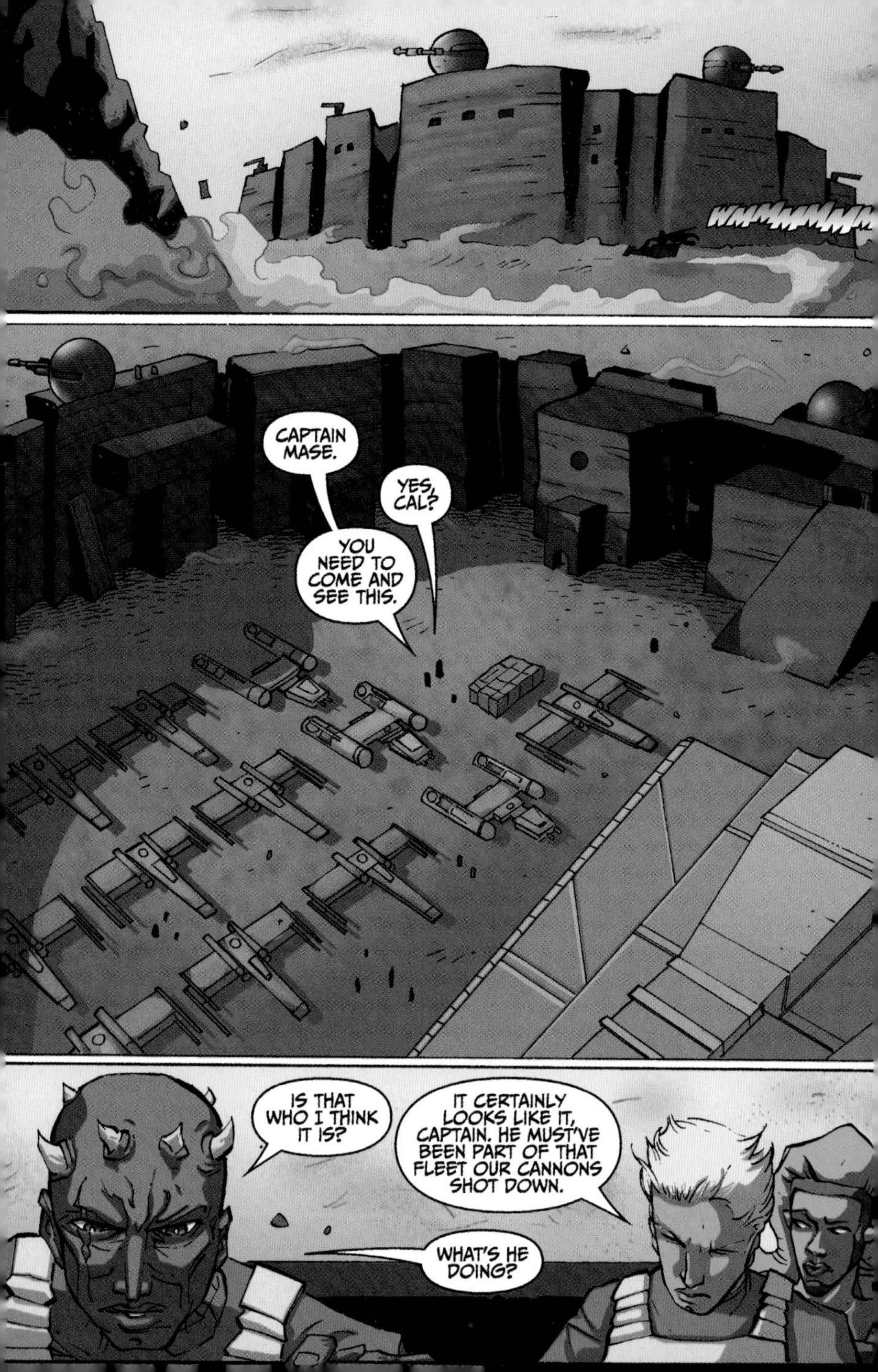
WHAMMMMMMM
CAPTAIN MASE.
YES, CAL?
YOU NEED TO COME AND SEE THIS.
IS THAT WHO I THINK IT IS?
IT CERTAINLY LOOKS LIKE IT, CAPTAIN. HE MUST'VE BEEN PART OF THAT FLEET OUR CANNONS SHOT DOWN.
WHAT'S HE DOING?

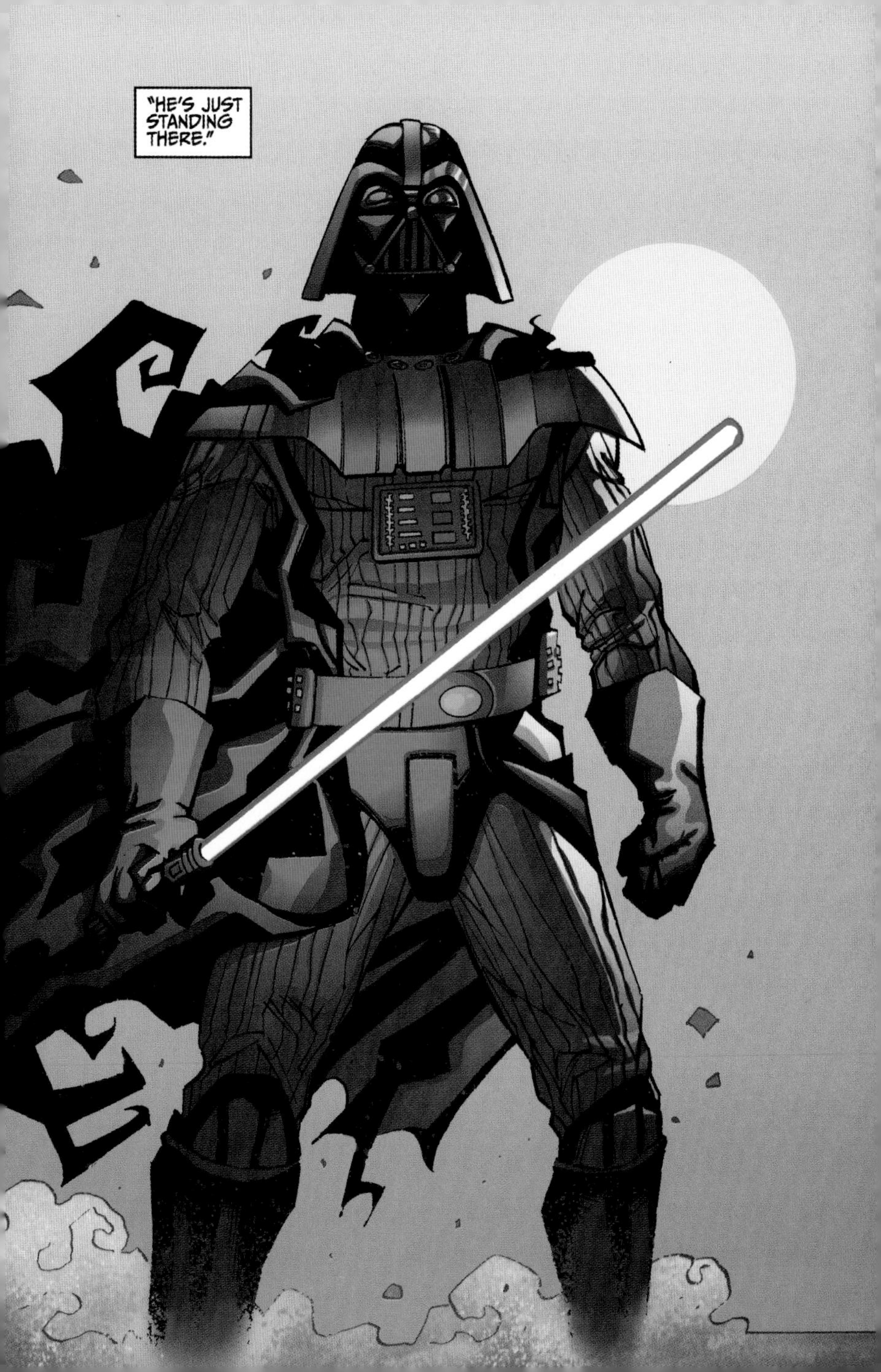
"HE'S JUST STANDING THERE."

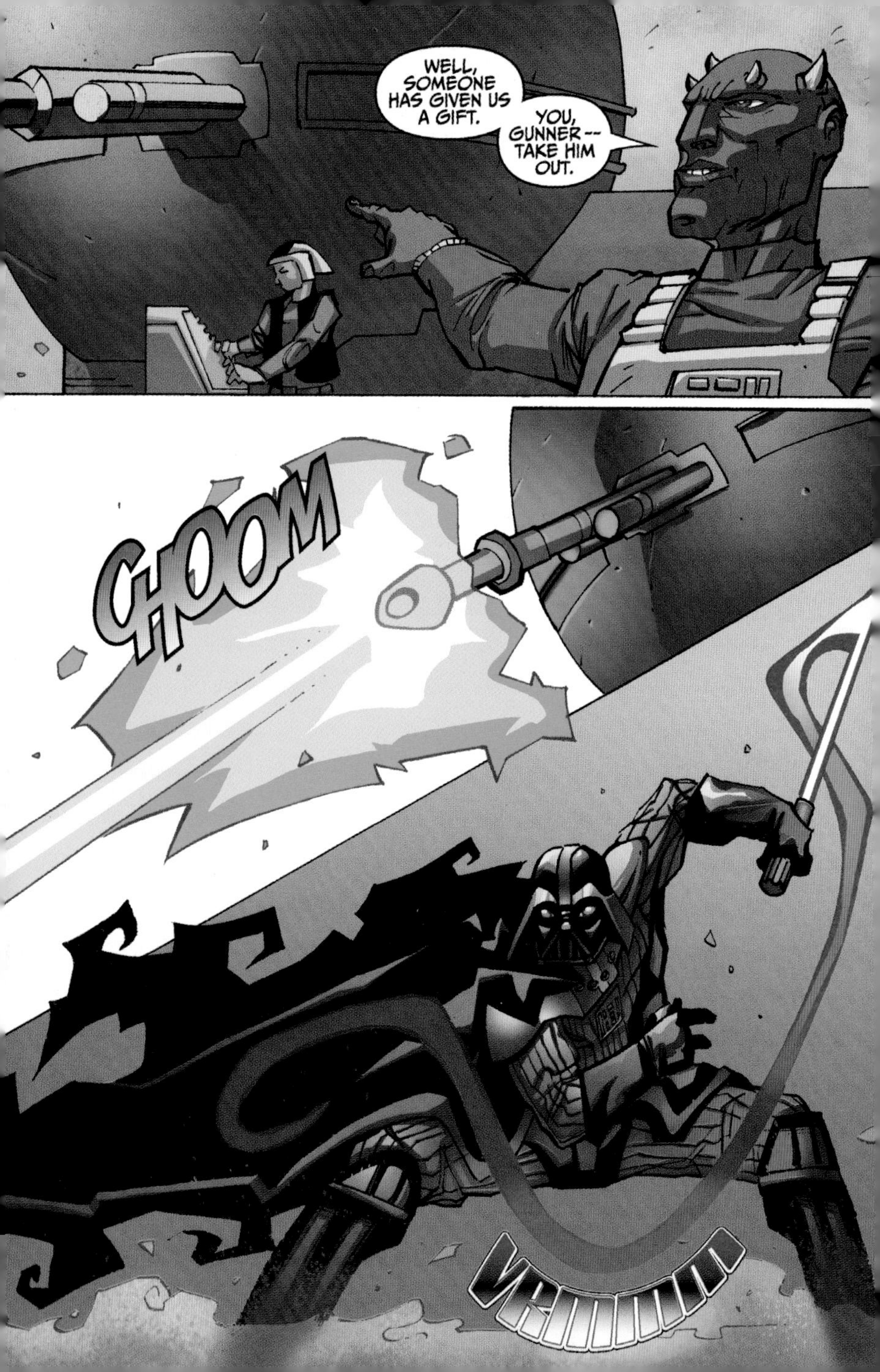
WELL, SOMEONE HAS GIVEN US A GIFT.
YOU, GUNNER-- TAKE HIM OUT.
CHOOM

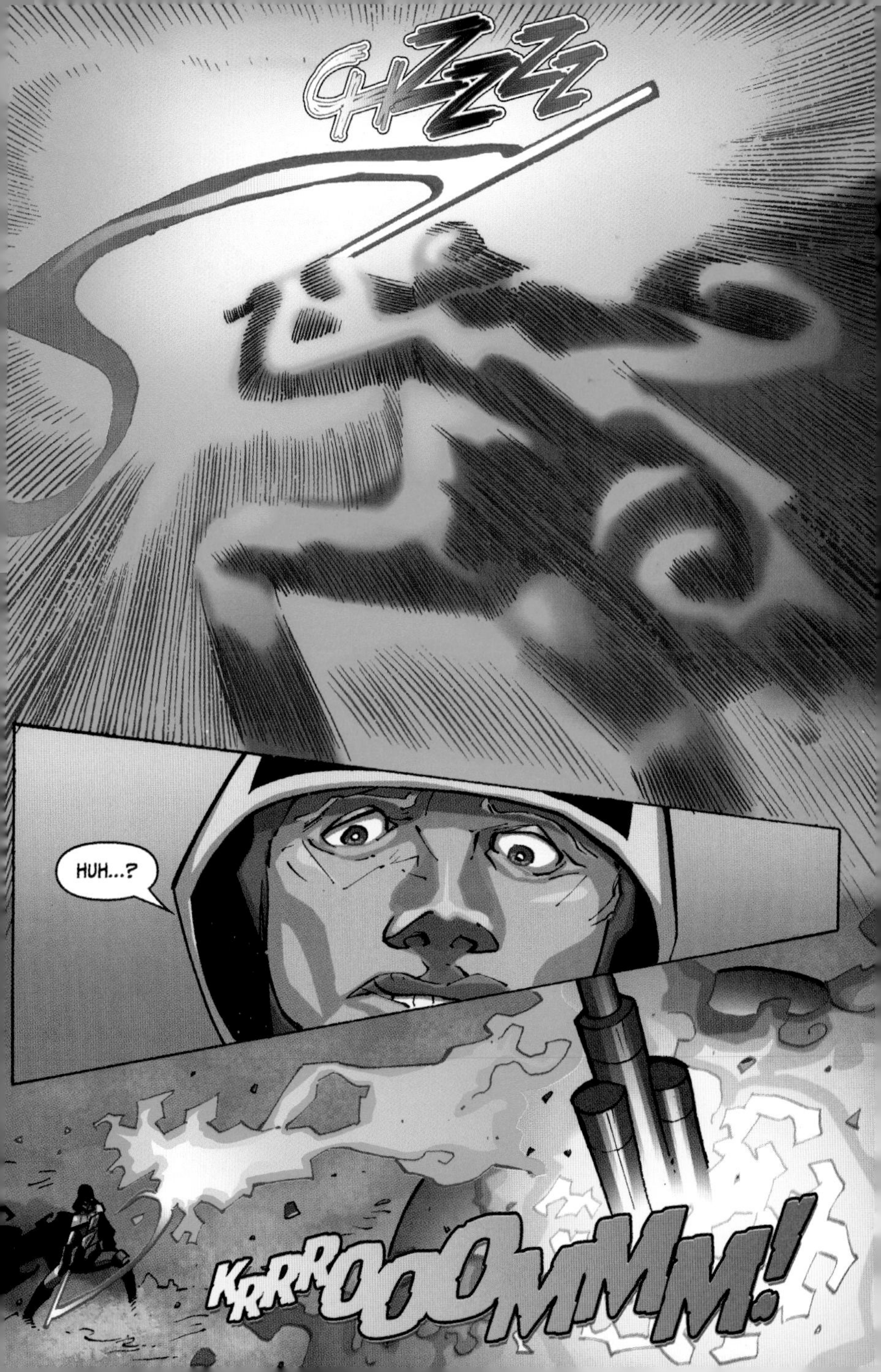
GHZZZZ
HUH...?
KRRRROOOMMMM!

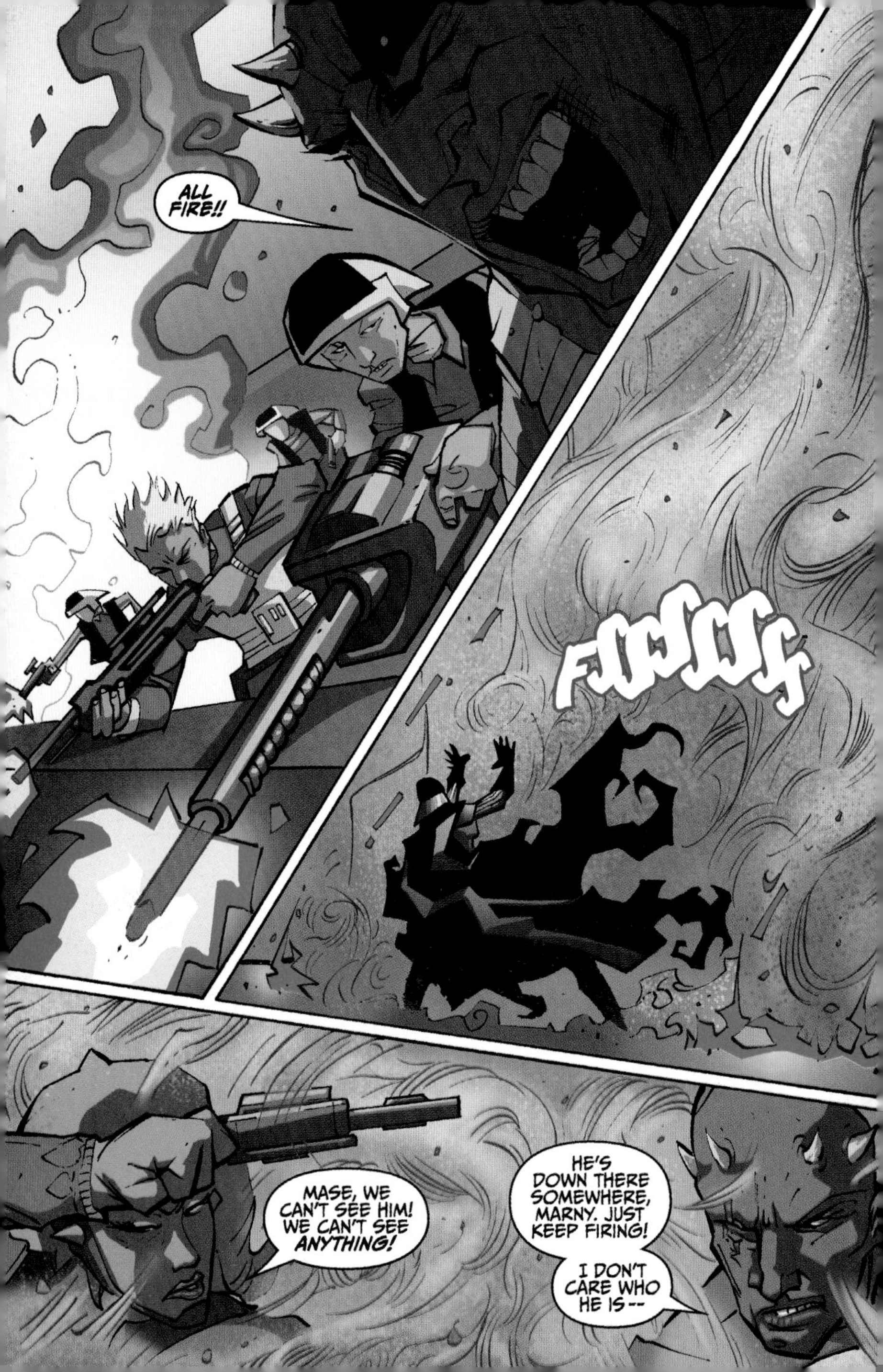
ALL FIRE!!
FOOSSSH
MASE, WE CAN'T SEE HIM! WE CAN'T SEE ANYTHING!
HE'S DOWN THERE SOMEWHERE, MARNY. JUST KEEP FIRING!
I DON'T CARE WHO HE IS--

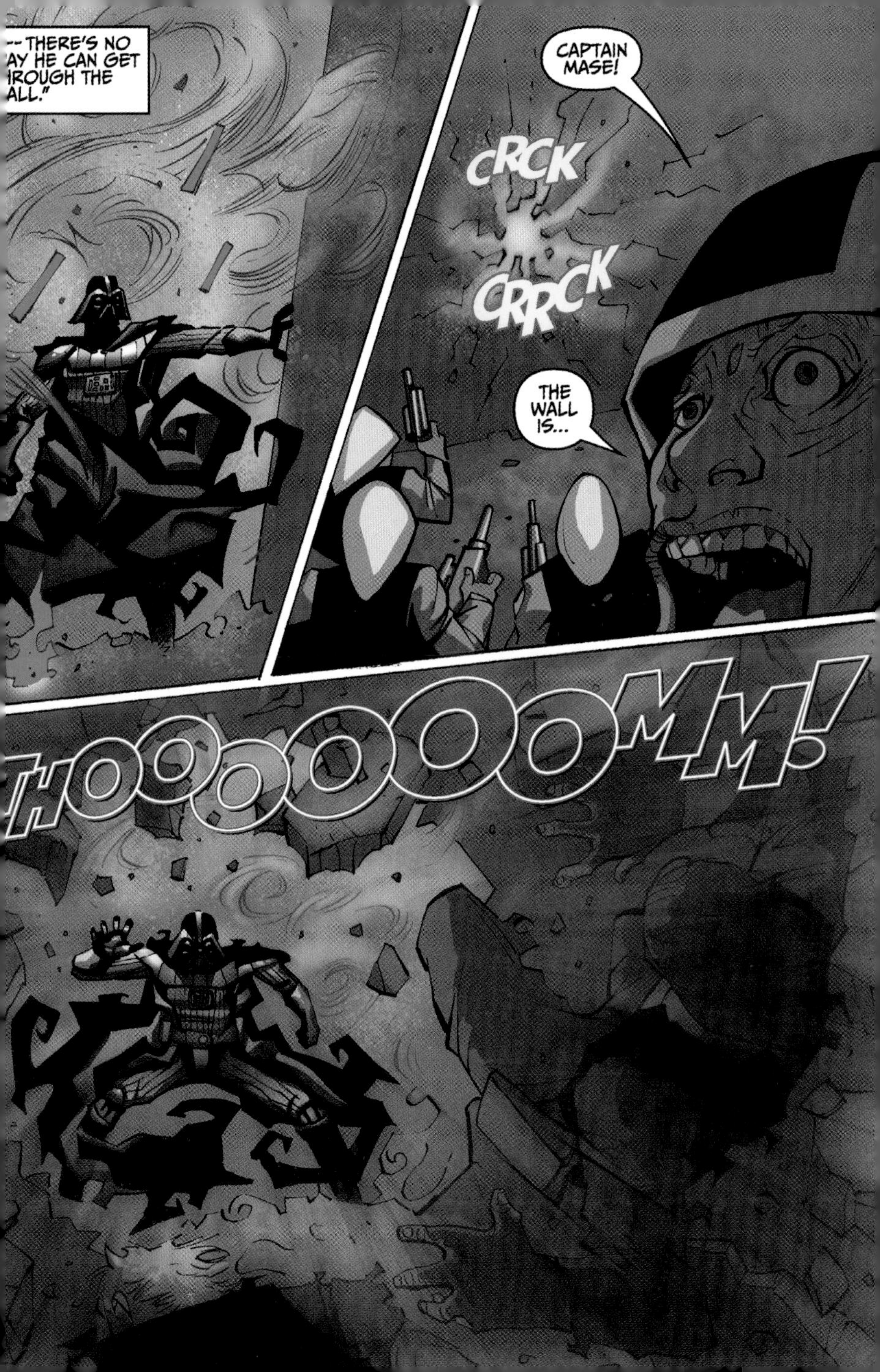
-- THERE'S NO
AY HE CAN GET
IROUGH THE
ALL."
CAPTAIN MASE!
CRCK
CRRCK
THE WALL IS...
HOOOOOOOMM!

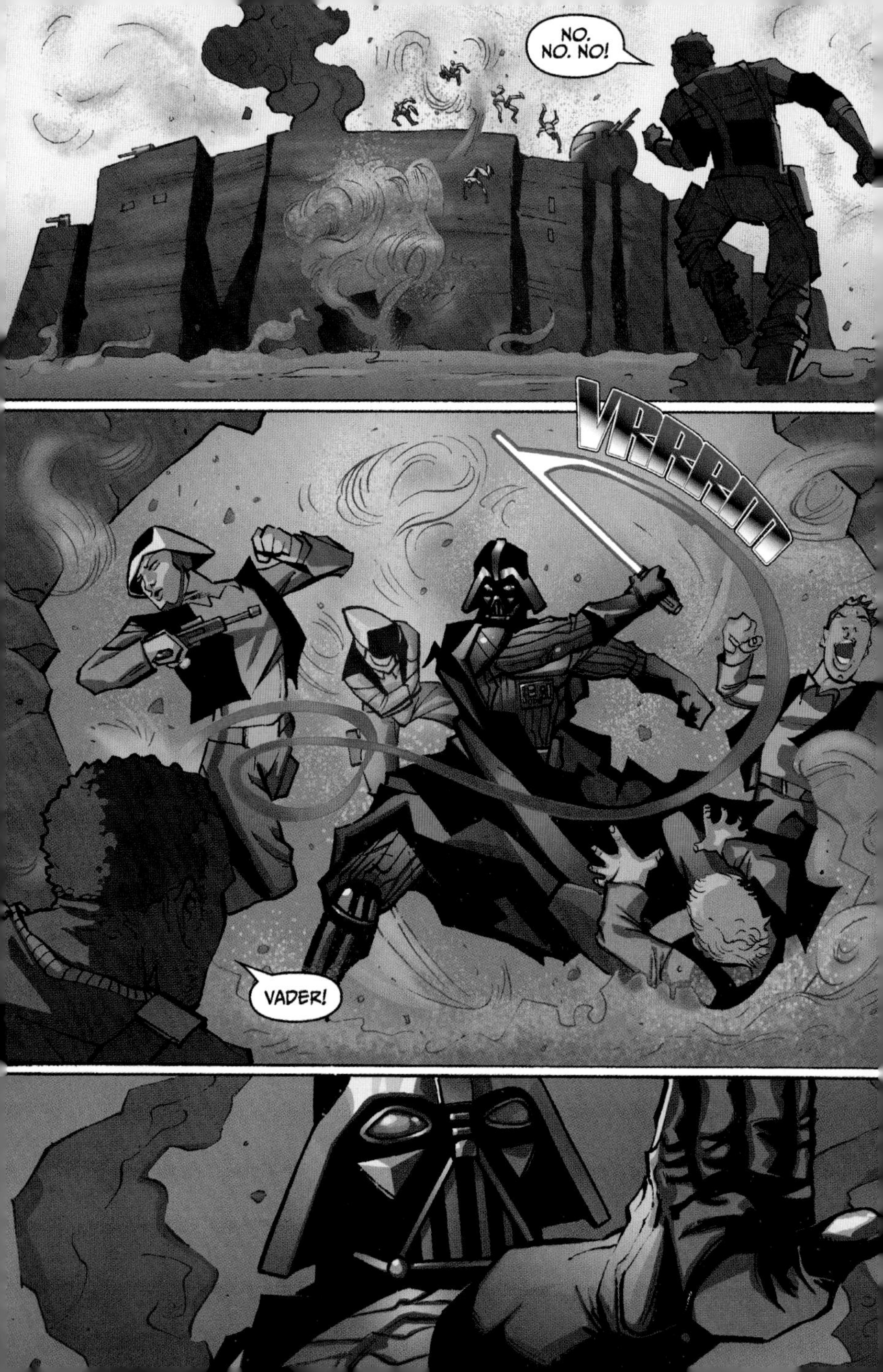
NO. NO. NO!
VRRRRM
VADER!

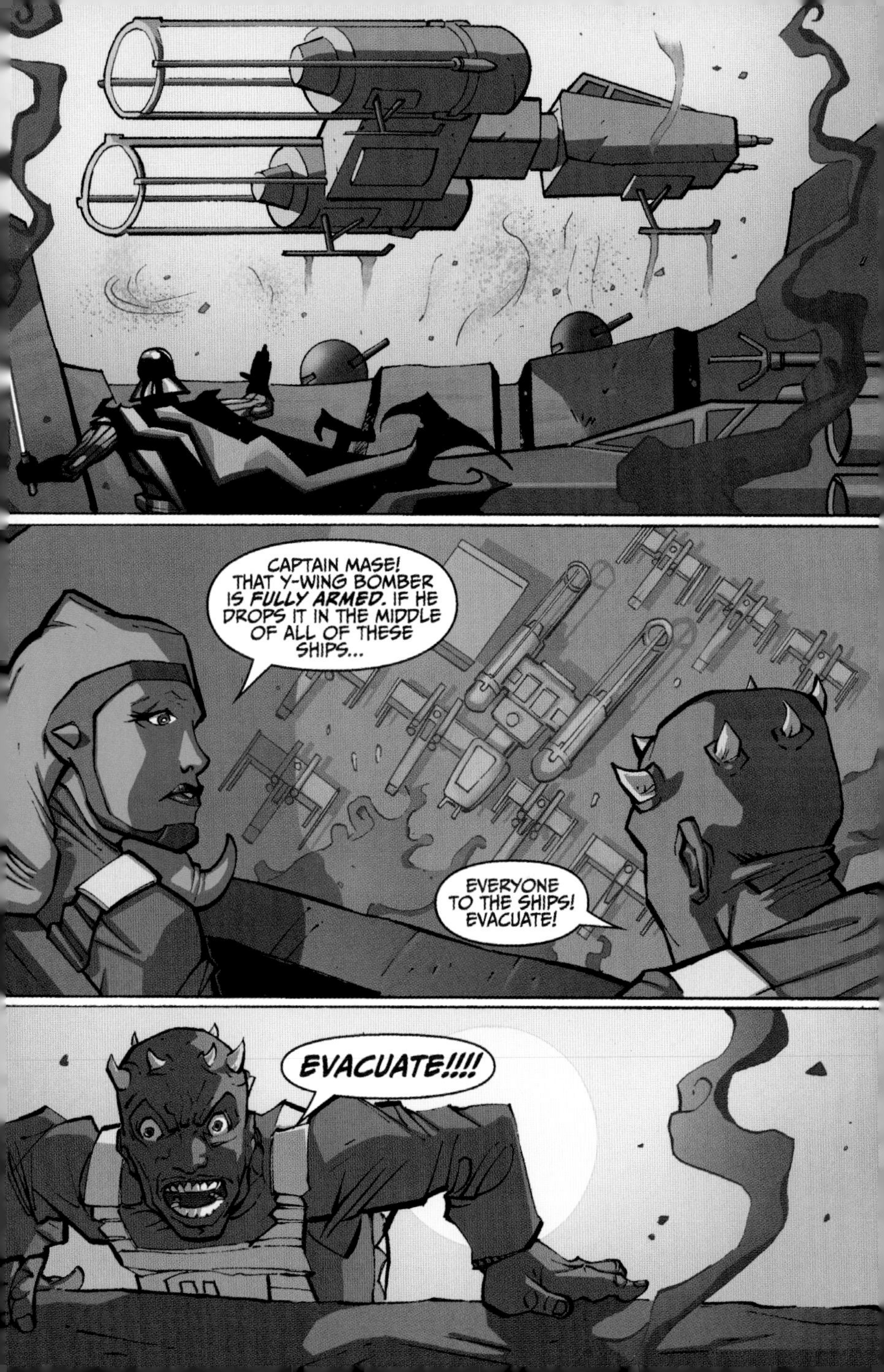
CAPTAIN MASE! THAT Y-WING BOMBER IS FULLY ARMED. IF HE DROPS IT IN THE MIDDLE OF ALL OF THESE SHIPS...
EVERYONE TO THE SHIPS! EVACUATE!
EVACUATE!!!!

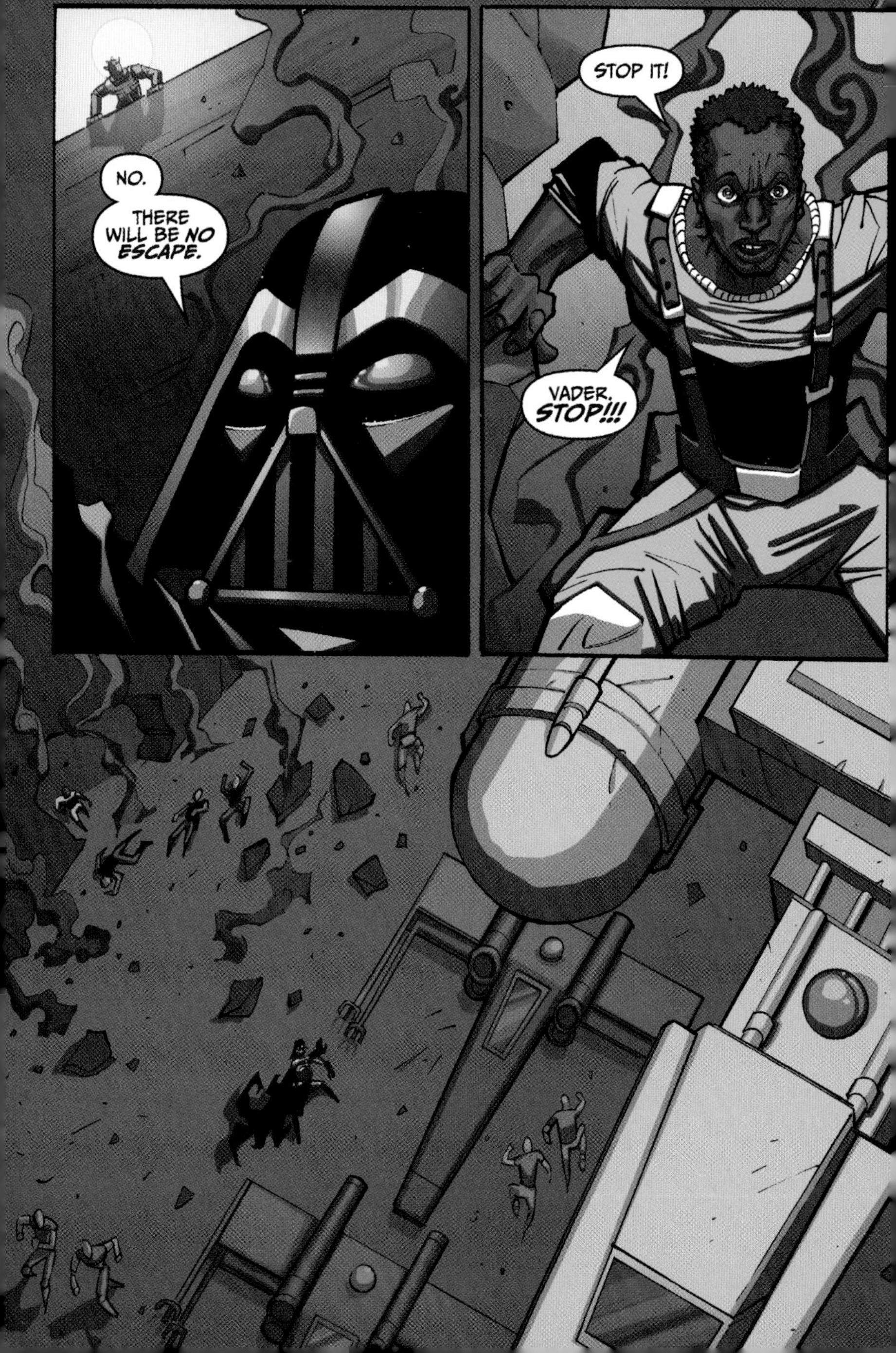
NO.
THERE WILL BE NO ESCAPE.
STOP IT!
VADER. STOP!!!

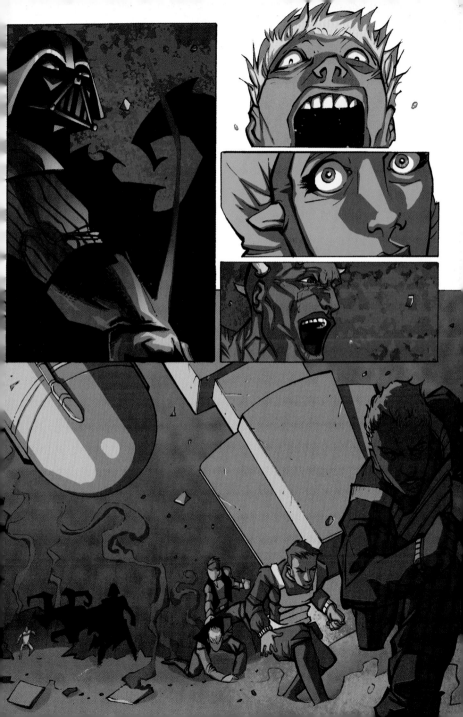

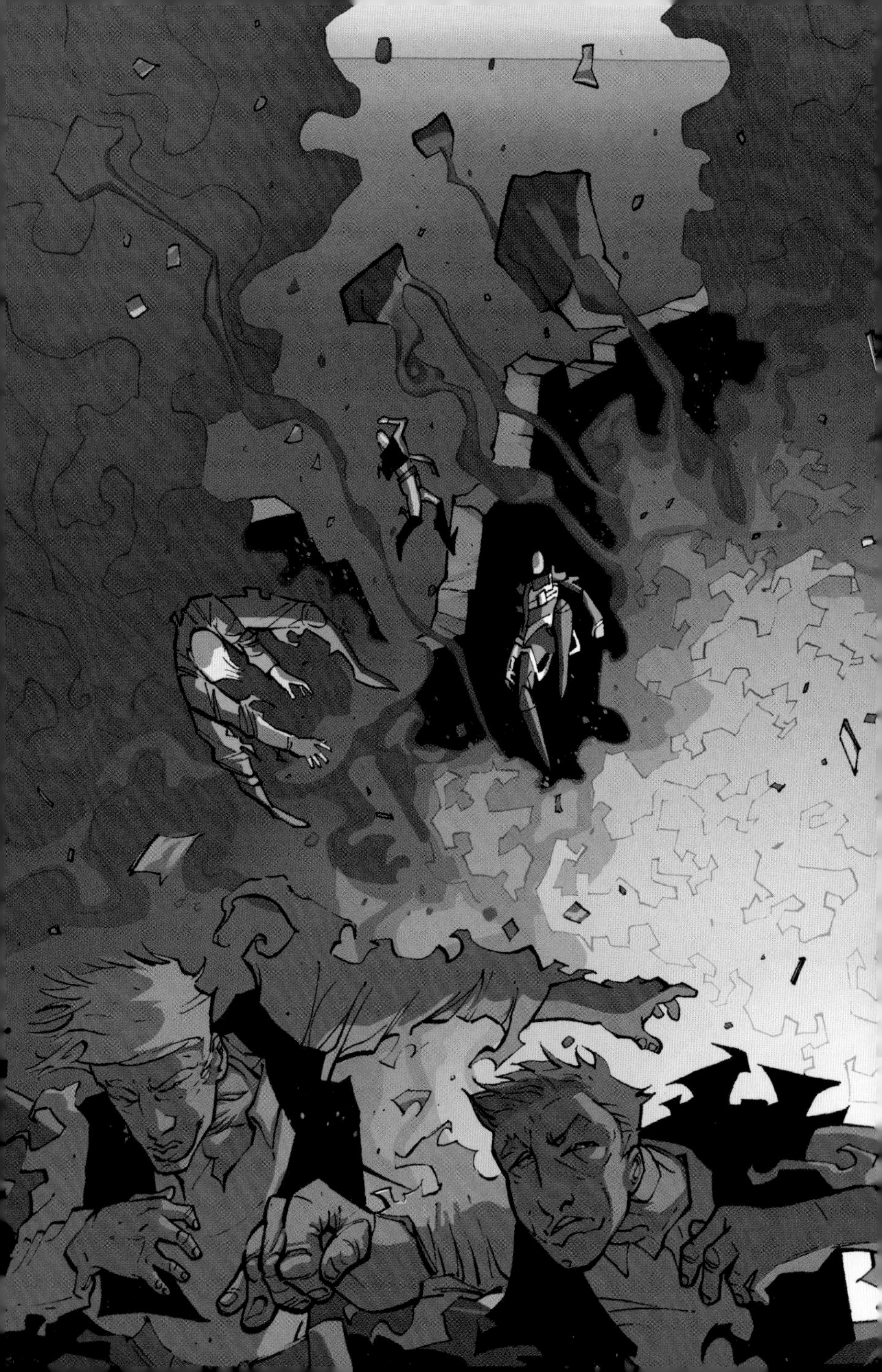

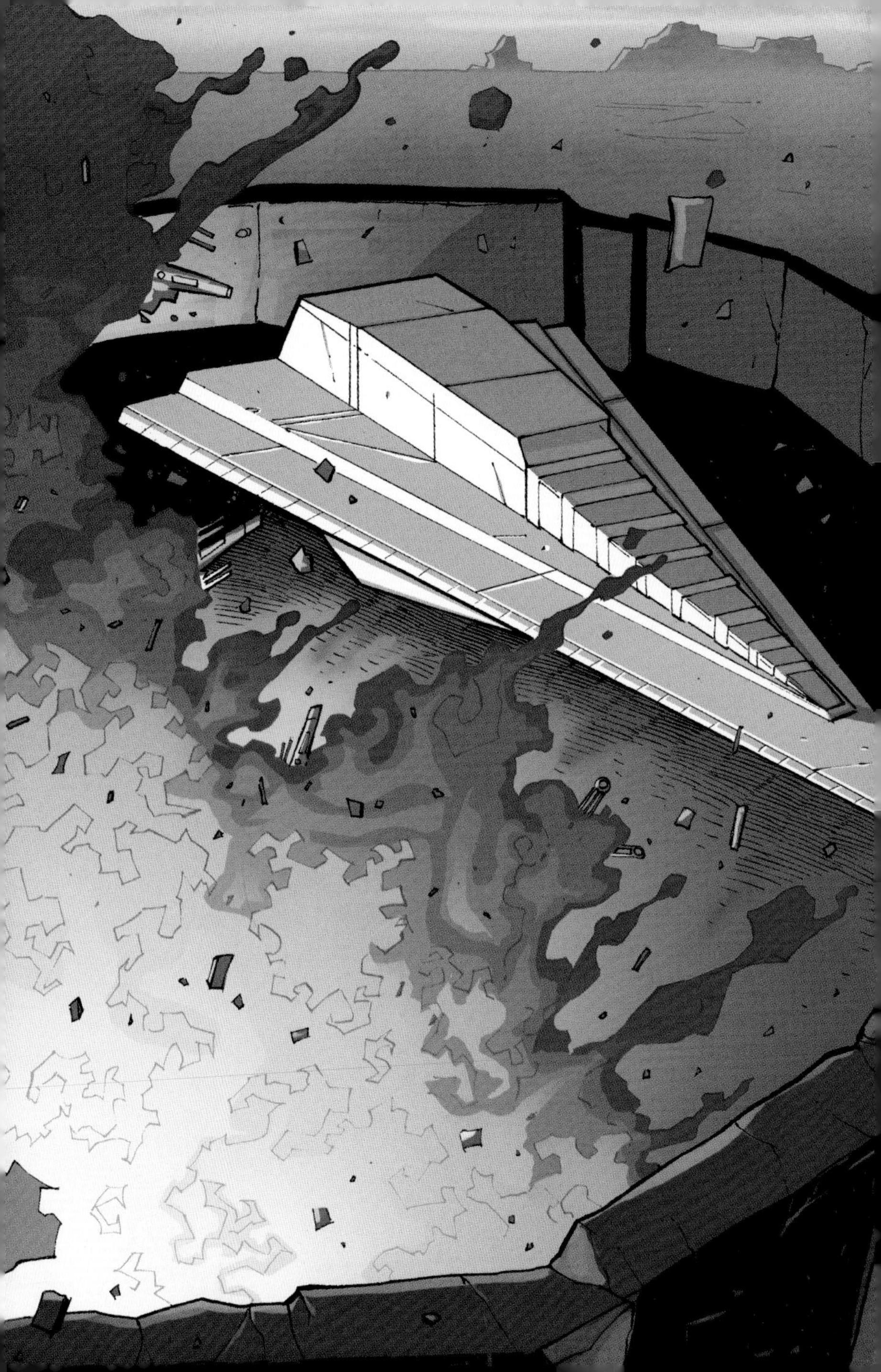

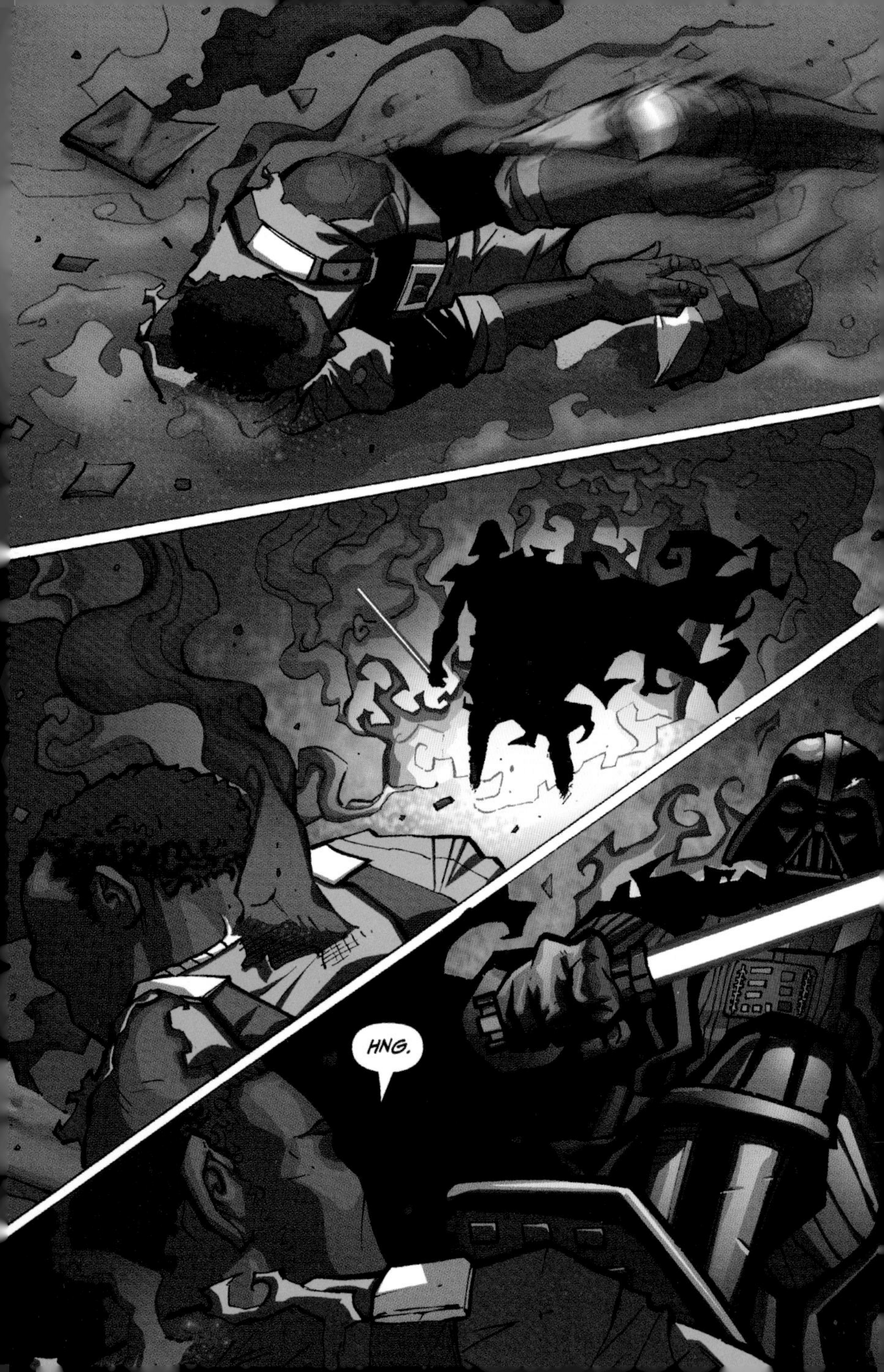
HNG.

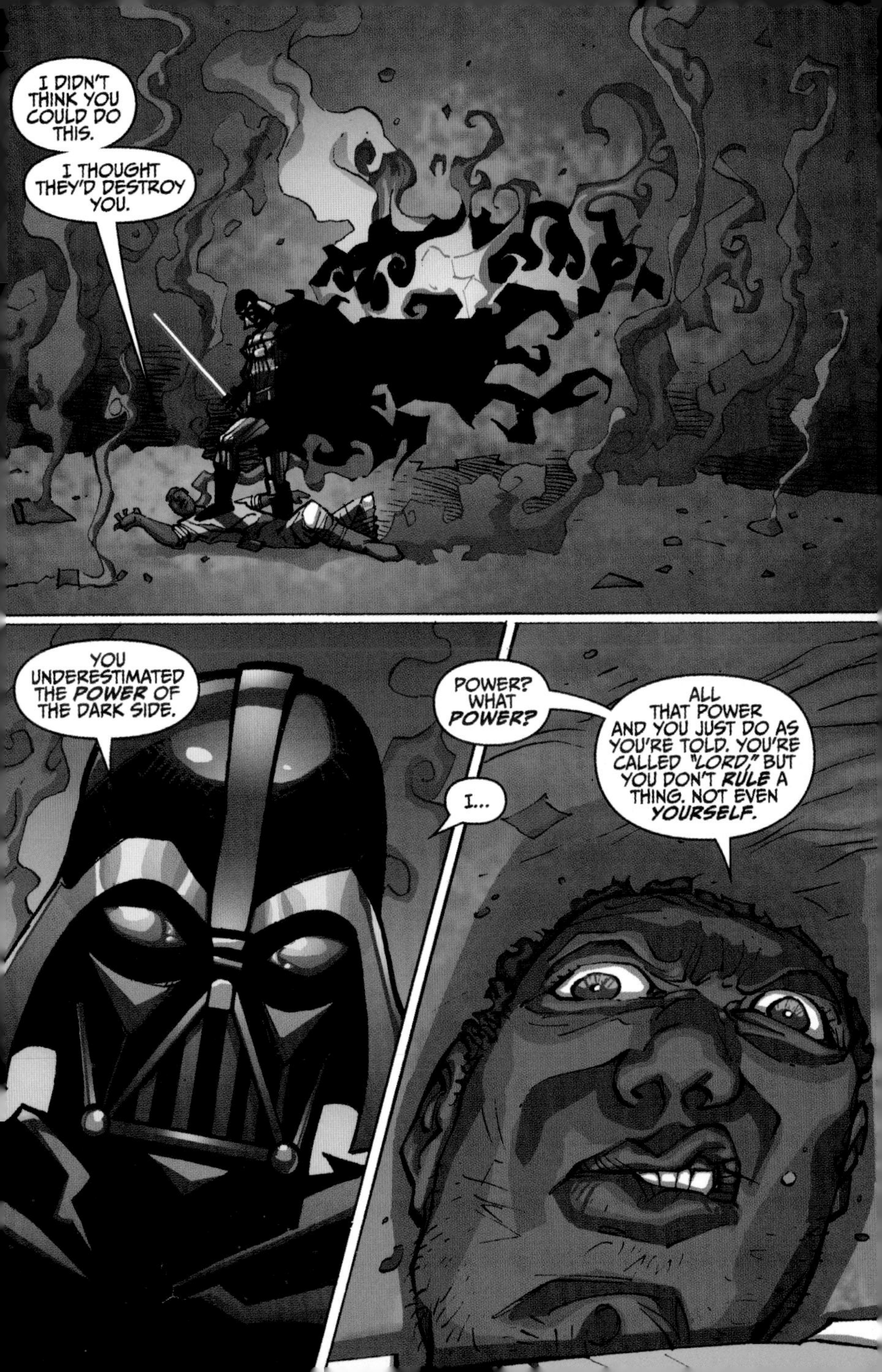
I DIDN'T THINK YOU COULD DO THIS.
I THOUGHT THEY'D DESTROY YOU.
YOU UNDERESTIMATED THE *POWER* OF THE DARK SIDE.
POWER? WHAT *POWER?*
ALL THAT POWER AND YOU JUST DO AS YOU'RE TOLD. YOU'RE CALLED *"LORD,"* BUT YOU DON'T *RULE* A THING. NOT EVEN *YOURSELF.*
I...

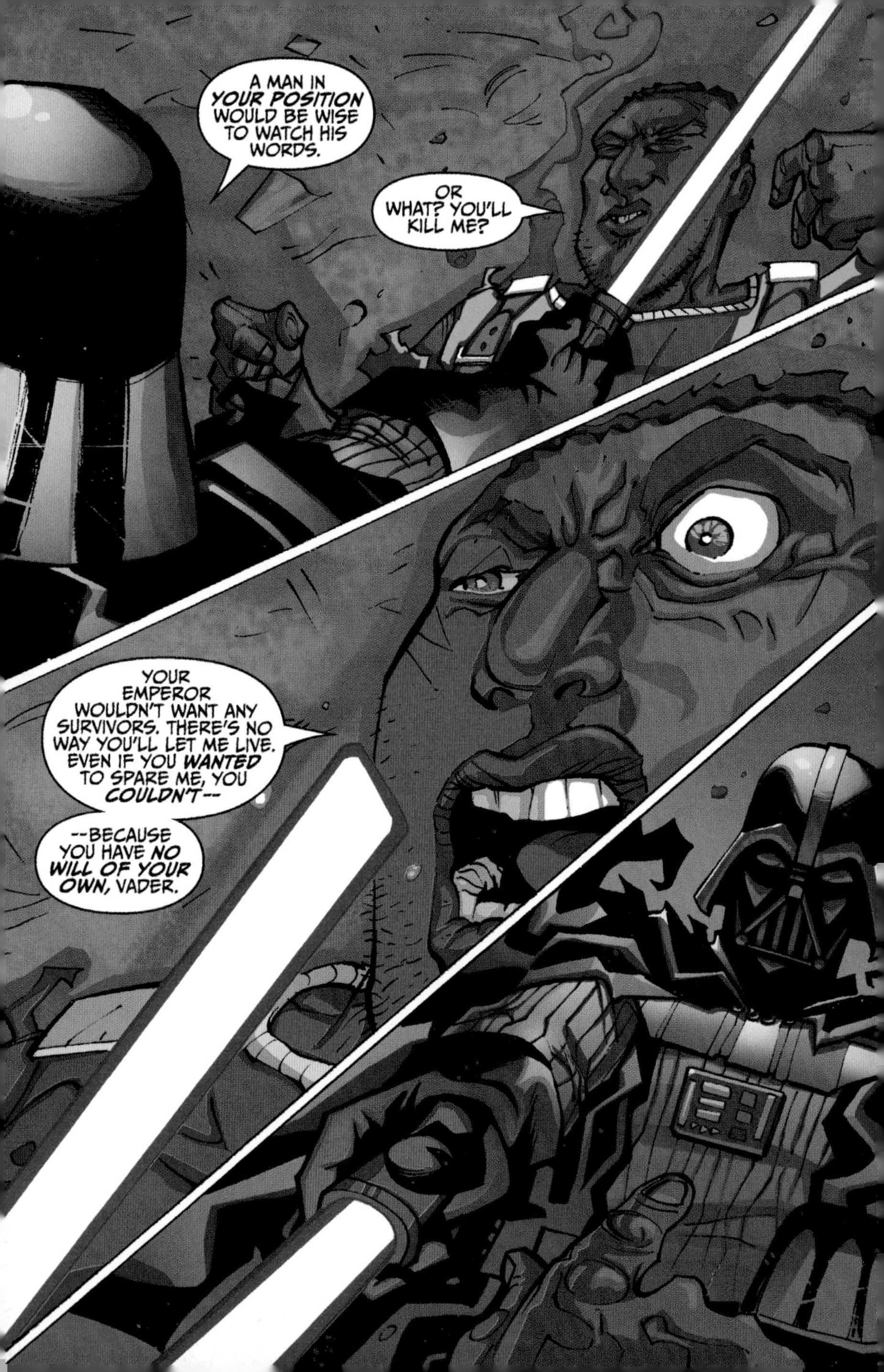
A MAN IN YOUR POSITION WOULD BE WISE TO WATCH HIS WORDS.
OR WHAT? YOU'LL KILL ME?
YOUR EMPEROR WOULDN'T WANT ANY SURVIVORS. THERE'S NO WAY YOU'LL LET ME LIVE. EVEN IF YOU WANTED TO SPARE ME, YOU COULDN'T--
--BECAUSE YOU HAVE NO WILL OF YOUR OWN, VADER.

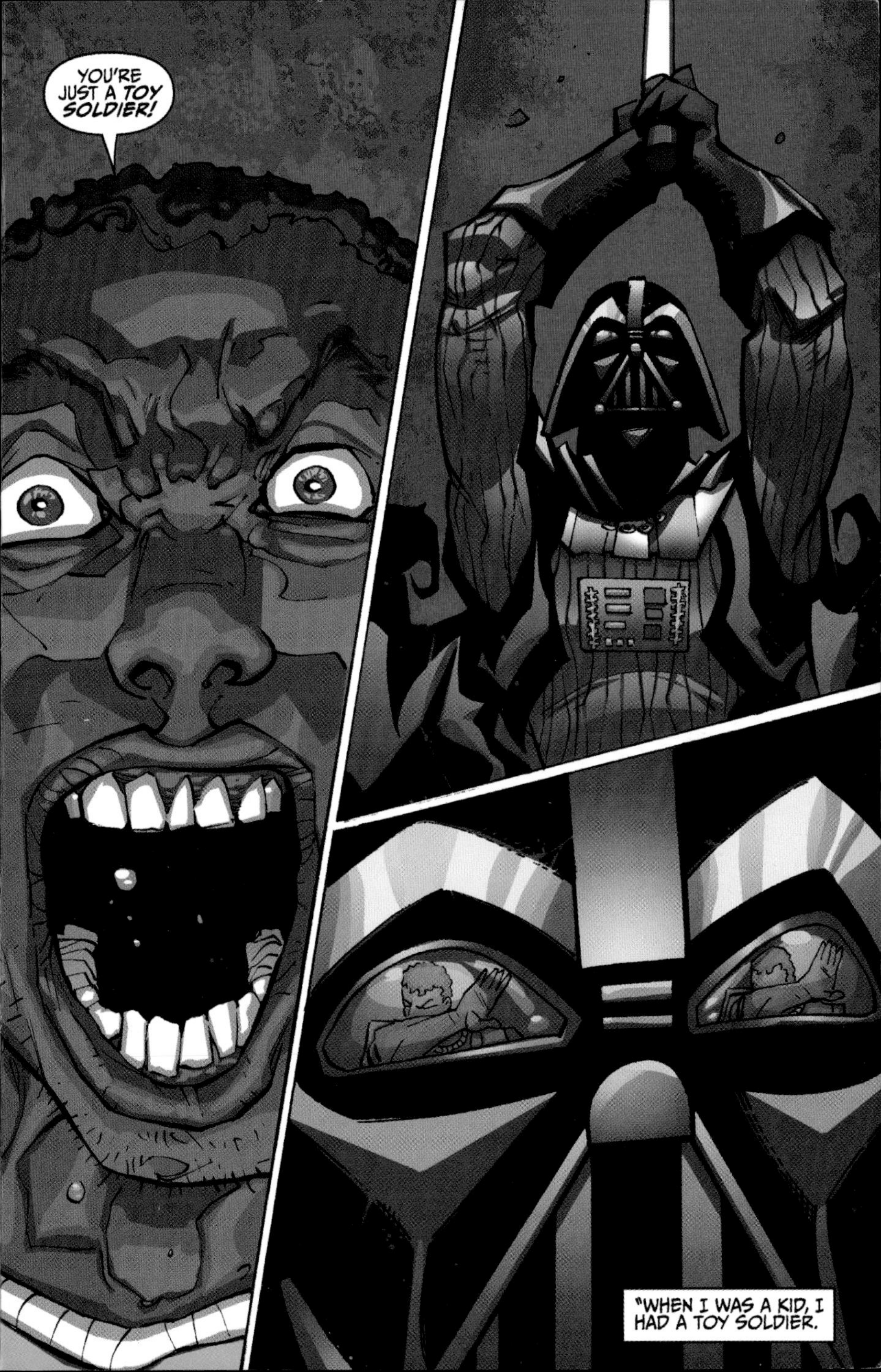
YOU'RE JUST A TOY SOLDIER!
"WHEN I WAS A KID, I HAD A TOY SOLDIER.

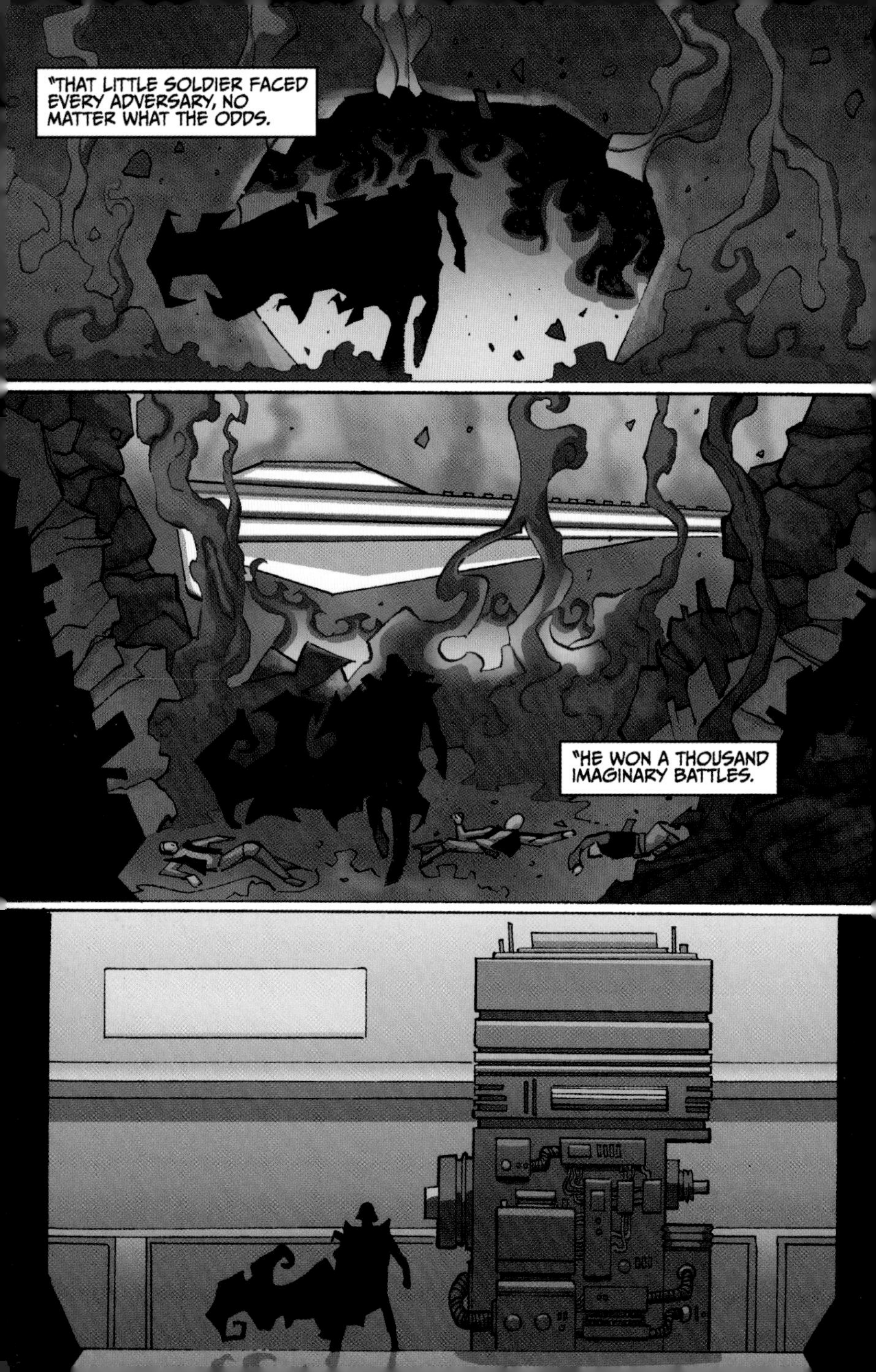
"THAT LITTLE SOLDIER FACED EVERY ADVERSARY, NO MATTER WHAT THE ODDS.
"HE WON A THOUSAND IMAGINARY BATTLES.

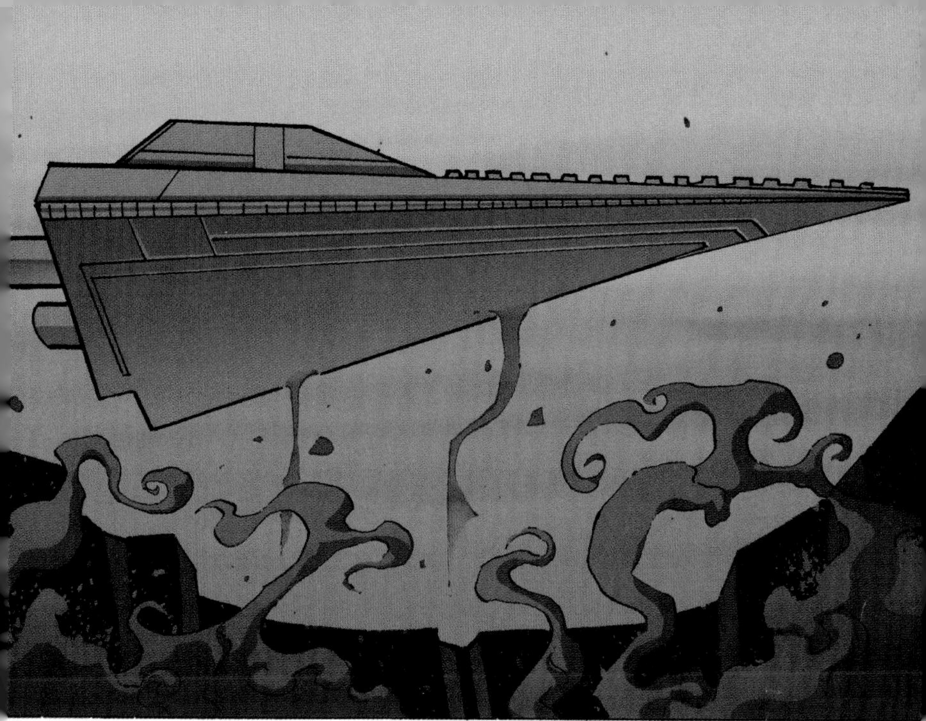

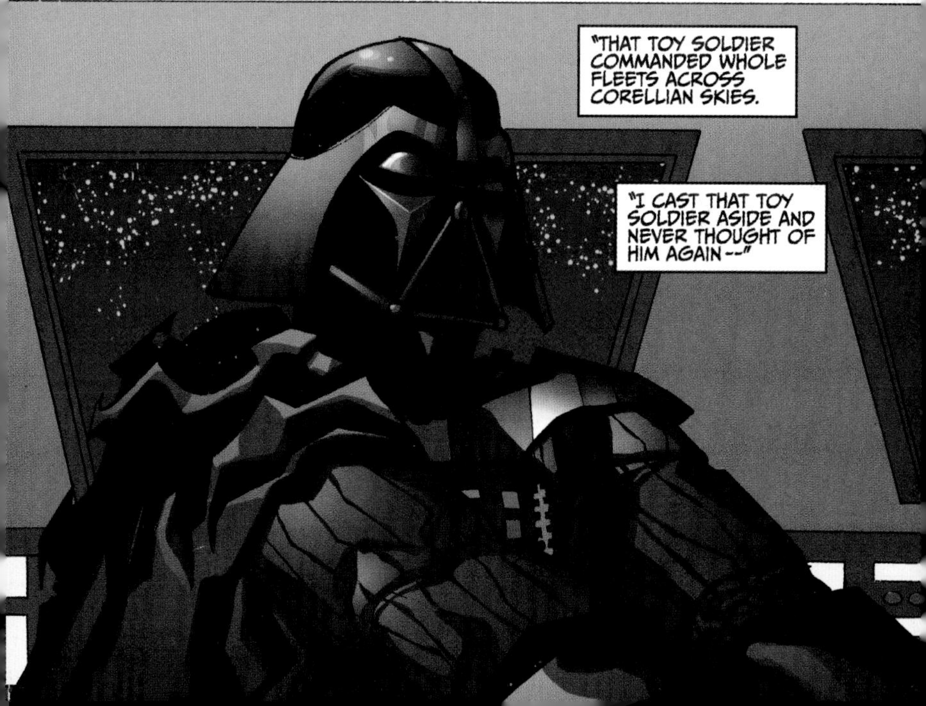
"THAT TOY SOLDIER COMMANDED WHOLE FLEETS ACROSS CORELLIAN SKIES.
"I CAST THAT TOY SOLDIER ASIDE AND NEVER THOUGHT OF HIM AGAIN--"

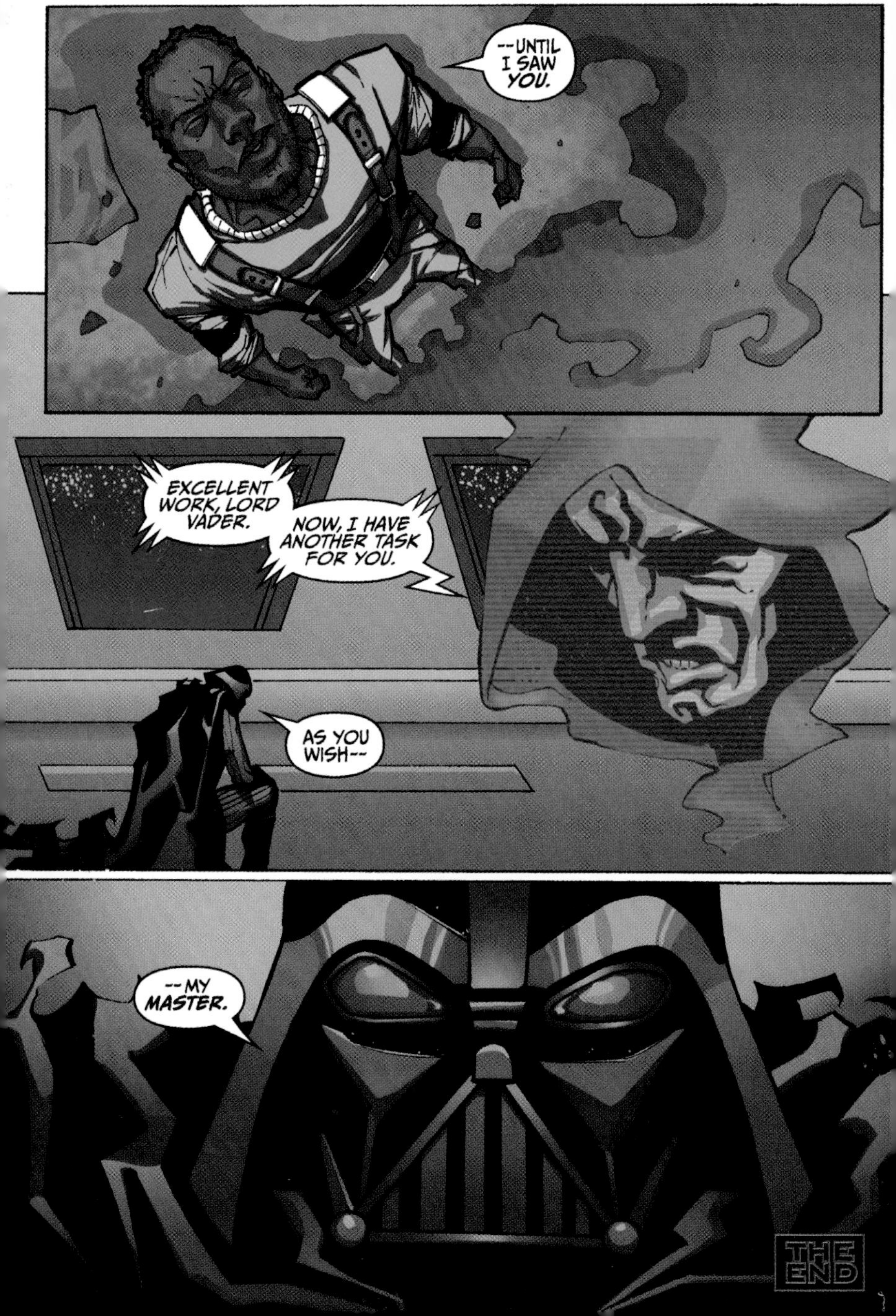
--UNTIL I SAW YOU.
EXCELLENT WORK, LORD VADER.
NOW, I HAVE ANOTHER TASK FOR YOU.
AS YOU WISH--
--MY MASTER.
THE END

President and Publisher **Mike Richardson**

Executive Vice President **Neil Hankerson**

Chief Financial Officer **Tom Weddle**

Vice President of Publishing **Randy Stradley**

Vice President of Business Development **Michael Martens**

Vice President of Marketing, Sales, and Licensing **Anita Nelson**

Vice President of Product Development **David Scroggy**

Vice President of Information Technology **Dale LaFountain**

Director of Purchasing **Darlene Vogel**

General Counsel **Ken Lizzi**

Editorial Director **Davey Estrada**

Senior Managing Editor **Scott Allie**

Senior Books Editor **Chris Warner**

Executive Editor **Diana Schutz**

Director of Design and Production **Cary Grazzini**

Art Director **Lia Ribacchi**

Director of Scheduling **Cara Niece**

STAR WARS GRAPHIC NOVEL TIMELINE (IN YEARS)

Omnibus: Tales of the Jedi—5,000–3,986 BSW4
Knights of the Old Republic—3,964–3,963 BSW4
Jedi vs. Sith—1,000 BSW4
Omnibus: Rise of the Sith—33 BSW4
Episode I: The Phantom Menace—32 BSW4
Omnibus: Emissaries and Assassins—32 BSW4
Twilight—31 BSW4
Bounty Hunters—31 BSW4
The Hunt for Aurra Sing—30 BSW4
Darkness—30 BSW4
The Stark Hyperspace War—30 BSW4
Rite of Passage—28 BSW4
Jango Fett—27 BSW4
Zam Wesell—27 BSW4
Honor and Duty—24 BSW4
Episode II: Attack of the Clones—22 BSW4
Clone Wars—22–19 BSW4
Clone Wars Adventures—22–19 BSW4
General Grievous—22–19 BSW4
Episode III: Revenge of the Sith—19 BSW4
Dark Times—19 BSW4
Omnibus: Droids—5.5 BSW4
Boba Fett: Enemy of the Empire—3 BSW4
Underworld—1 BSW4
Episode IV: A New Hope—SW4
Classic Star Wars—0–3 ASW4
A Long Time Ago . . . —0–4 ASW4
Empire—0 ASW4
Rebellion—0 ASW4
Boba Fett: Man with a Mission—0 ASW4
Omnibus: Early Victories—0–3 ASW4
Jabba the Hutt: The Art of the Deal—1 ASW4
Episode V: The Empire Strikes Back—3 ASW4
Shadows of the Empire—3.5 ASW4
Episode VI: Return of the Jedi—4 ASW4
Mara Jade: By the Emperor's Hand—4 ASW4
Omnibus: X-Wing Rogue Squadron—4–5 ASW4
Heir to the Empire—9 ASW4
Dark Force Rising—9 ASW4
The Last Command—9 ASW4
Dark Empire—10 ASW4
Boba Fett: Death, Lies, and Treachery—10 ASW4
Crimson Empire—11 ASW4
Jedi Academy: Leviathan—12 ASW4
Union—19 ASW4
Chewbacca—25 ASW4
Legacy—130–137 ASW4

Old Republic Era
25,000 – 1000 years before
Star Wars: A New Hope

Rise of the Empire Era
1000 – 0 years before
Star Wars: A New Hope

Rebellion Era
0 – 5 years after
Star Wars: A New Hope

New Republic Era
5 – 25 years after
Star Wars: A New Hope

New Jedi Order Era
25+ years after
Star Wars: A New Hope

Legacy Era
130+ years after
Star Wars: A New Hope

Infinities
Does not apply to timeline

Sergio Aragonés Stomps Star Wars
Star Wars Tales
Star Wars Infinities
Tag and Bink
Star Wars Visionaries

BSW4 = before *Episode IV: A New Hope*. ASW4 = after *Episode IV: A New Hope*.

STAR WARS®
CLONE WARS ADVENTURES

Don't miss any of the action-packed adventures of your favorite STAR WARS® characters, available at comics shops and bookstores in a galaxy near you!

STAR WARS
CLONE WARS
ADVENTURES
Vol 4
STAR WARS
CLONE WARS
ADVENTURES
Vol 1
THREE NEW STORIES! ALL-JEDI ACTION!
STAR WARS
CLONE WARS
ADVENTURES
Vol 10
JEDI, CLONES, DROIDS, AND BOUNTY HUNTERS IN FOUR FANTASTIC TALES!

$6.99 each!

Volume 1
ISBN 978-1-59307-243-8

Volume 2
ISBN 978-1-59307-271-1

Volume 3
ISBN 978-1-59307-307-7

Volume 4
ISBN 978-1-59307-402-9

Volume 5
ISBN 978-1-59307-483-8

Volume 6
ISBN 978-1-59307-567-5

Volume 7
ISBN 978-1-59307-678-8

Volume 8
ISBN 978-1-59307-680-1

Volume 9
ISBN 978-1-59307-832-4

Volume 10
ISBN 978-1-59307-878-2

AVAILABLE AT YOUR LOCAL COMICS SHOP OR BOOKSTORE
To find a comics shop in your area, call 1-888-266-4226
For more information or to order direct: • On the web: darkhorse.com • Phone: 1-800-862-0052 Mon.–Fri. 9 AM to 5 PM Pacific Time.
• E-mail: mailorder@darkhorse.com *Prices and availability subject to change without notice.